Unbelieving Children *and the* Parents Who Love Them

Michael J. Fanstone

VINE
BOOKS

SERVANT PUBLICATIONS
ANN ARBOR, MICHIGAN

Vine Books is an imprint of Servant Publications especially designed to serve evangelical Christians.

Published by Servant Publications
P.O. Box 8617
Ann Arbor, Michigan 48107

Cover design: Eric Walljasper

01 02 03 10 9 8 7 6 5 4 3

Printed in the United States of America
ISBN 1-56955-181-2

LIBRARY OF CONGRESS CATALOGING-IN-PUBLICATION DATA

Fanstone, Michael J. (Michael John), 1948-
  Unbelieving children and the parents who love them / by Michael Fanstone.
    p.   cm.
  Includes bibliographical references and index.
  ISBN 1-56955-181-2 (alk. paper)
  1. Parents—Religious life. 2. Adult children—Religious life. 3. Ex-church members—Family relationships. I. Title.

BV4529.F34 2000
248.8'45—dc21   00-040819

Contents

Acknowledgments / 7

Introduction / 9

1 God Will Empathize With Your Pain / 11

2. God Will Help You to Understand His Plans / 31

3. God Will Forgive and Heal Past Problems / 43

4. God Will Work Through You As You Persistently Pray / 65

5. God Will Shine Through Your Witness / 85

6. God Will Help You to Invest Spiritually in Your
   Grandchildren / 109

7. God Will Use You in Your Church / 127

Notes / 149

Further Reading / 153

Scripture Index / 155

Acknowledgments

M ost projects of any value are a team effort, and this book
is no exception. As well as those who so helpfully (and
anonymously) provided the stories and statistical information I
have cited, I want to thank Mari Thompson for proofreading
the manuscript as it evolved and for making numerous recom-
mendations as to how I could improve it. Dr. Raymond Brown,
my former Principal and church history tutor from Spurgeon's
College, London, helped by pointing me in the right direction
when I was searching for relevant historical examples to cite. I
am very grateful to him. In addition, Helen Motter, whom I
have never met because we live on opposite sides of the Atlantic
Ocean, was commissioned by Servant Publications to edit my
material. As we exchanged numerous e-mails over the months,
Helen contributed many valuable suggestions that I believe will
help this publication to be used more effectively by God. What
a team!

Finally, I want to record my thanks to my wife, Diane, and
our youngsters, Becky and Stephen, for their support and
patience while I have shut myself away in order to write this
material. I am also grateful to the church that I serve as pastor,
Emmanuel Baptist Church in Gravesend, Kent, England, for
allowing me a sabbatical leave, during which most of the work
was done.

Last, but not least, if there is teaching, encouragement, and
inspiration here that helps you and your family, then please join

me in thanking the Lord, who gave me the vision, time, and energy to put it together in the first place. My prayer is that in the years ahead God will bring to himself the adult children of many committed Christians. If at some stage you have good news to share, I would be so glad to hear from you via the publishers.

Michael J. Fanstone

Introduction

Across the world millions of parents are sad. This is not because their children have grown up and flown the nest. They were expecting that to happen. Rather, parents are grieved that their children have abandoned the Christian faith they were introduced to at an early age. Despite the loving nurture of Christian parents and a supportive church, many youngsters regrettably fall away from Christ during adolescence or later.

The suffering of parents whose children have rejected the faith is even worse if they have taken seriously the admonition of Proverbs 22:6: "Train a child in the way he should go, and when he is old he will not turn from it." Such parents inevitably find themselves consumed with pain and guilt as they struggle to understand what they did wrong. They find no comfort in knowing that other youngsters brought up in Christian homes around the world have made the same choice.

Other parents feel sad because they themselves came to faith later in life and therefore had no opportunity to raise their children to become Christians. They now wonder if there is any serious prospect of their grown-up children ever turning to Christ. They would dearly love that to happen, but they feel powerless to influence their adult children in matters of faith.

The reasons young people fall away are, of course, numerous and complex. Often human influences alone may be responsible, since the world we live in encourages youngsters to establish their own individual values rather than adopting those of their parents or the Bible.

We cannot ignore, however, the influence of the unseen spiritual realm in their lives.

Satan works hard to hinder the progress of God's work. The more the world's attractions or the deliberate advance of evil can draw youngsters from what is godly, the better he likes it. Satan probably smiles contentedly every time a child or young person brought up in a Christian family misses an opportunity to make a lifelong decision to follow Jesus Christ.

In any situation of this kind there is hope, however, because God is committed to seeing his work grow. Furthermore, every parent has a part to play in God's plans for his or her children. Even if you are in your nineties and your offspring are in their sixties or seventies, you still have a vital role to play in their lives! Despite the fact that your children may be independent adults in their own right, God calls you, the parent, to work in partnership with him so that your children will have the opportunity to come into his kingdom.

God's call and challenge to you is to catch his vision and cooperate with him so that ultimately your whole family can share in the glorious experience of being in heaven with him for eternity. Although the circumstances in every family differ, this book aims to help you become God's partner in a demanding but incredibly important task. Each chapter will show you how God can work in and through your life to bring your grown children to Christ.

Michael J. Fanstone
Gravesend, England, 2000

One

❦

God Will Empathize
With Your Pain

The situation was not going to be easy for Rose and Peter to handle, and they knew it. James, their fifteen-year-old son, had just declared his intention not to attend church anymore. He had gone to church with his parents his whole life, but he now refused. It was boring, he said.

His parents could not understand his feelings. After all, he had recently enjoyed a skiing weekend in the mountains with the young people from the church, and a few months earlier they had all spent a fun week together at the coast. Rose and Peter admitted that their Sunday worship services could be a little predictable and dry, but they just could not grasp why James suddenly wanted to cut all ties with the church.

What made it worse was that their daughter, who was three years older than James, had done the same thing at his age. A sweet and sensitive girl, Karen had never found it easy to make friends, so when she came home one day and announced that she was going out with Claire, a girl she worked with at her

Saturday job, Rose and Peter were delighted. They did not know, however, that Claire's upbringing had been very different from Karen's and that the new friendship would begin to steer Karen away from her parents' values.

Less than two months later Karen declared that she would not be attending church anymore. Claire had gradually convinced her that religion was phony and that all churches really wanted was people's money. Nothing Rose and Peter could say would make any difference. Karen had not been back to church since. Her parents were deeply hurt, but they tried to get over it.

When James made his announcement, all their feelings over Karen's earlier decision came rushing back. Now Rose and Peter were struggling under a heavy load of guilt and pain as questions swirled in their minds. What had they done to deserve this? Was God angry with them? What would people at church think? Had they failed as parents? Would their children ever be saved now? These questions plagued them through many unhappy days and disturbed nights.

Plunged Into Sadness

Rose and Peter are by no means unique. The trauma they experienced has been repeated millions of times over the centuries. No end of households have been plunged into sadness by non-negotiable decisions made by children—often much younger children than Karen and James. Each time this happens it provokes a heart-wrenching response in the parents, who know in that moment their family has just suffered a serious spiritual setback.

Short of picking up their children by the scruff of the neck, depositing them in the car, and throwing them into church, there is a limit as to how much Christian parents can do at this point. In a sense it is too late. From now on the parents have to recognize that circumstances have changed. This demands a hard and painful mental readjustment.

Alice and Jim have had years to make such a readjustment. In their early seventies now, they are approaching their golden wedding anniversary. They became Christians in their mid-twenties, when their first child was a toddler. Alice had made friends with her next-door neighbor, a committed Christian, and soon Alice was a believer too.

It took Jim almost two more years before he dedicated his life to Christ, although he started to attend church at the same time as Alice. As a consequence Jim and Alice brought their children up to go to church and to accept the Christian faith. They were thrilled when their first three youngsters made professions of faith and joined the church. However, their fourth child, Jody, never did accept Christ and left the church soon after becoming a teenager. Sadly, as time went by, the other children followed, drifting away from the church in their late teens or early twenties.

All that happened over a quarter of a century ago, but Alice and Jim have never forgotten it. Their family is now widely scattered, and they see three of their children and their families only once or twice a year. Jody still lives with her husband and children in the same town in which she was raised, so Alice and Jim are able to spend more time with her.

Excluding God

While Alice and Jim are grateful that the relationship with all their children and grandchildren is solid, they remain very much aware that the children they brought up to love and honor God are completely excluding him from their lives. Any anger Alice and Jim once felt has dissipated. They now recognize that their anger was initially provoked by their embarrassment over suddenly having to go to church without their family. When it first happened, others in the church kept asking where their youngsters were, but after a while this ceased to be a topic of conversation.

Alice in particular breathed a sigh of relief at not having to talk about it anymore, but the pain and disappointment inside her remained as potent as ever. To this day she remains grieved over her children's spiritual condition. She feels they are missing out on many of the good things that God wants to give them.

Interestingly, Jim's response is different. Having been brought up by his ambitious father to seek success in life, he wanted each of his own children to accomplish a set of goals he felt were important. Among these was the expectation that each of his children would follow their parents' example and become Christians who serve God faithfully and are fully committed to a local church.

When his youngest daughter abandoned the church, Jim was deeply disappointed, but he could cope with one failure balanced by three successes. As the years passed and one by one the other three rejected God and the church, Jim became increasingly discouraged. He took their rejection of God personally, and although his children were all successful in their chosen careers and family life, he perceived himself as a spiritual and parental failure.

His first response to his disappointment was to become depressed for weeks on end. Then, because he felt helpless to redeem the situation and could not cope with his depression, he began to block out his feelings. Now he rarely thinks about it. For more than twenty years he has hardly given a moment's thought to his children's spiritual condition. He knows that if he opens the door to the pain again, it will make his otherwise happy retirement miserable. Since he is not prepared for that to happen, he keeps his pain safely locked away in a hidden compartment of his mind.

God Comes Alongside

The situations these couples have had to face are just two examples of the wide range of painful circumstances that exist in many Christian homes and lives. This book will attempt to minister to them all. Whatever pain you are carrying, God wants to come alongside and help you.

How he can do this will become more apparent when we have seen how God himself responds when subjected to pain. We will begin, however, by identifying the range of emotional responses parents feel when their children abandon the faith in which they have been brought up. Six reactions seem to be commonplace: disappointment, anger, hurt, frustration, guilt, and a deep sense of failure. Let's examine each of these reactions separately.

Disappointment

Like Jim, most parents dream of what they would like their children to become. Whether or not parents have openly discussed their dreams with their children, when a child fails to fulfill those parental expectations, disappointment sets in, bringing with it a whole set of negative emotions.

How would you feel if one of your children failed to live up to your expectations? Imagine, for example, that you had carefully taught your son or daughter important and clear-cut principles such as to work hard, be honest, be responsible with money, treat others with respect and to accept personal responsibility. Later on, however, you discovered that he or she had been expelled from university for cheating in exams or stealing from a fellow student. How would you respond?

Without a doubt you would be absolutely horrified because some of your prime expectations for your offspring had been instantly ripped to shreds. To say you would be disappointed would be a gross understatement. No doubt your reaction would be much the same if your son or daughter decided to abandon Christianity and the church. I trust it never happens to you, but regrettably, other families have had this bombshell descend upon them. Each incident provokes great sadness.

Disappointment is debilitating. It produces negative feelings and attitudes and in some people can lead to depression. Even in people who are normally positive, disappointment can dramatically reduce their sense of encouraging expectation. Disappointment digs deeply into a person's sense of well-being.

Anger

The differences in our personalities mean that different things trigger different reactions in us all. Interestingly, what makes you sad may not incite any noticeable reaction in me. What provokes me to anger may reduce you to tears. As any parent knows, the actions and attitudes of our children from their earliest days can draw from us some of our deepest responses.

By no means do all Christian parents become angry when their children abandon the faith they were brought up to believe in. Some parents do, however. They feel slighted and offended themselves but also incredulous that their children, after all the Christian nurture they have received, would dare treat their loving heavenly Father in such an outrageous way.

After all, he has showered them with goodness and kindness since they were conceived. He brought them safely into this world. He provided a loving and fairly stable environment in which to grow up. They had the additional benefit of a church family supporting them as they passed through childhood and adolescence. Precious resources have been lavished on them as church workers have loved them and guided them, praying and trusting that in due course they would become loyal, mature servants of God.

In addition God himself has been faithful through the long teenage years as they struggled to find their own identity. He has provided direction as they have come to the end of their high school education. Many have found a fulfilling career and may have identified the partner with whom they intend to spend the rest of their life.

In view of all this and more, parents may find themselves arguing with some indignation with a child who has announced that his churchgoing is history. Their anger may rise up as they demand to know what right their child has to do this. What makes their child think that he or she can simply throw out God and his church like yesterday's newspaper?

Giving up. Jerry and Monica were certainly amazed when their daughter Kerry told them she would not be going to church the next Sunday or, as far as she could see, ever again. Earlier they had been relieved that Kerry seemed to have sailed through the transition years when some young people abandon the church and God.

As far as they knew, Kerry, now eighteen, had never made a personal commitment to Jesus Christ, but she did seem to be well entrenched within the church youth group. Jerry and Monica found this reassuring.

What offended them most when Kerry told them her news, however, was the blasé way in which she explained it. She made it sound as if God had never meant anything to her and that she was not at all sure now that he existed. Additionally, in a sweeping condemnation that deeply hurt Jerry and Monica, Kerry criticized not only her peers but also some of the church's leaders whom she had known for years. That night Jerry and Monica felt as if the bottom had fallen out of their world. They were furious with their daughter and felt deeply wounded.

There are dangers here to be aware of. Writer Larry Crabb, in his book *Men and Women*, observed that human beings find anger a difficult emotion to handle and all too easily either deny its extent or find its cause in someone else.[1] We instinctively try to avoid facing up to the real issues whenever we can. Because of our natural tendency to be self-centered, we become defensive and protective when we feel threatened.

When we find ourselves in a situation that arouses anger within us, we need to do two things as soon as we can. First, we must face up to the real issues that provoked the emotion in the first place. Second, we must ensure that we deal with our anger thoroughly so that no residue is left to provoke a feeling of resentment.

Anger and resentment often exist in close proximity. While anger may at first be a natural and healthy response, if it is not dealt with and resolved, it can burrow into a person's life and take up permanent residence. Resentment toward the person with whom we feel angry can grow, and once firmly rooted, it tends not to dissipate until the original problem of anger is acknowledged, confronted, and dealt with.

Janet knows this only too well. She and her husband, both leaders in their church, felt highly embarrassed when their son, then thirteen, refused point-blank to go to church with them anymore. For over four years Janet locked up the anger inside, and many of her family and friends noticed that she had become moody and sullen.

Only recently did Janet feel ready to receive counseling. Now, having forgiven her son, she regrets the years she wasted because of her unwillingness to face what was really going on inside of her. At last she senses she is making some welcome progress.

Hurt

Like you, I get hurt when something aimed at me hits me square on. In my case that isn't likely to be a physical blow. People who engage in contact sports or are in the armed forces have to deal with physical pain inflicted by others. But the hurts most adults experience are more often from emotional blows. Attitudes, words, looks, and body language are all ways that others can use to communicate hurtful messages to us. Even though we haven't been hurt physically, we can be left reeling emotionally when hit where we are most vulnerable.

Tony and Hilary have been wounded spiritually and emotionally four times, by each of their children in turn. Not having been Christians long when their first child arrived, they brought their daughter up as best they could to believe in and trust Jesus. They followed a similar pattern with each of their children and genuinely expected them to become dedicated and loyal Christians.

One by one, however, their children drifted from the church during their teenage years. Despite Tony and Hilary's continuing prayers, none of their children seem remotely interested in the faith their loving parents have tried to live out at home. When other people's children seem to come effortlessly to trust Jesus, Tony and Hilary are left confused and not a little hurt. Still, they continue to pray that their children may ultimately find Christ.

Frustration

Some of the couples whose stories I told earlier felt frustration on top of their other emotions when their children abandoned God and the church. Frustration always sets in when we find ourselves helpless to change a situation.

Rose and Peter's frustration stemmed from their inability to grasp why James would want to disassociate himself from the church. It seemed to them that the church had contributed a great deal that was positive to his life, and his decision simply did not make sense to them, any more than Karen's had earlier. Each seemed to be based on a very shortsighted view, one that both young people would later regret bitterly.

Why their children could not see the wonderfully rich nature of God's love for them, they did not know. Why they were unafraid to step into an unknown future without the reassuring presence of the Good Shepherd, they could not imagine. Why they would not accept God's free grace, forgiveness, and the prospect of an eternal home in heaven, they simply could not grasp.

To Rose and Peter these seemed like irrational and irresponsible decisions. If possible they would have overruled them and sent Karen and James straight back to church. Their inability to do so with children who were nearly adults left them agitated and upset.

"I get so wound up inside," Rose explained to Peter one night. "I used to be able to direct where the children went, for how long, and what time they should get home. I had their present and, I thought, their future under control. Now James just laughs at me if I suggest he reconsider coming to church on Sunday."

"You don't expect me to take God and church seriously at *my* age, do you?" he asked his mother, in a tone that left no doubt as to what he expected the answer to be. Rose found it all very hard to cope with.

Guilt

It is not at all uncommon for Christian parents whose children are not growing spiritually to feel guilty before God. They think they have let him down. They believe that their witness and lifestyle cannot have been spiritually dynamic enough to convince their children their faith was authentic. After all, many parents have had a dozen or more years to let God shine through their lives at home, and it seems not to have been enough.

If you suffer from feelings of guilt, you know that guilt can have a debilitating impact on your life. If you take your faith seriously but now feel that you have let God down, the one who has been so wonderfully faithful to you, it can make you feel terribly uncomfortable in his presence. Some Christians have even felt too unworthy to continue attending church.

Cathy and Dave fall into this category. Their only son, George, made a seemingly sincere profession of faith when he was fourteen and was baptized soon afterward. At first George took an active part in the youth work of their family church. Then he became increasingly involved in recreational interests, and these gradually eroded his attendance at any church-related meetings. By the time he was sixteen, his connection with the church was virtually nonexistent.

His parents took this badly. They had recognized many gifts of leadership and communication in George that could, if developed, make him a dynamic Christian leader in the future. They had never mentioned this to him but had prayed regularly that he would fulfill all the plans God had for his life. Now their hopes and dreams for their only son seemed shattered, and they kept wondering what they should have done to help him stay close to God.

In Cathy and Dave's situation, there is some reality about their response. Five or six years earlier their marriage had gone through a rocky spell, and their family life had been very unstable for two or three years. They knew at the time that they ought to get some help but never did, and their problems rumbled on. Now they recognize, albeit too late, that they undoubtedly hindered their son's spiritual progress while all this was happening. As they cannot rewind the clock, what they need now is release from the guilt that weighs them down.

The good news, as we shall see later, is that God can free us from guilt, whether real or imaginary. The former, as in Cathy and Dave's case, is where our failure constitutes a genuine sin, which we need to repent of before God in order to be forgiven. Imaginary guilt, on the other hand, is felt by a Christian who feels snowed under by a general sense of unworthiness and uselessness. Satan often tries to impose such undeserved guilt on believers in order to undermine their faith.

Of course, every Christian has sinned and continues to sin. Each believer needs to confess and repent regularly. Satan's ploy, however, makes Christians feel bad, yet when they ask God what they have done to feel this guilt, they get no clear-cut answers. They simply cannot find any specific wrongdoing with which God is displeased. We shall see in chapter 3 what action is needed to break free from such feelings of false guilt.

A Deep Sense of Failure

Most new mothers and fathers begin their parenting career having had the experience of growing up with their own parents. In assessing that experience, they decide what was good, solid, and wise parenting and what they want to change when it is their turn. When babies are born into families, the parents have high hopes about the kind of children their parenting skills will produce.

In many cases parents presume, rightly or wrongly, that their offspring will grow up believing in the same things they have chosen themselves. Interestingly, they imagine their children to be versions of themselves, except that, having the benefit of their parents' experience and wisdom to draw on, they will make fewer mistakes and therefore will be more perfect chips off the old block.

Among the factors parents seem to forget is that culture changes from one generation to another. Our children and their offspring experience a far different world than the one we grew up in. For decades Western culture has been changing more and more rapidly. The pace of technological advance has contributed substantially to this increasing rate of change.

However, it may be the moral climate that has changed most since we were kids. In biblical times and for centuries afterward, parents and the wider family made the major contribution to a child's upbringing. Now parents seem to have unwittingly handed over to anyone and everyone else the task of raising their children. They allow not only the schools, but movies, TV, and, more recently, computer software programs and the Internet to make a significant impact on their children's lives.

The worst feature of this is that those who now often exert the greatest influence over our children and grandchildren have goals that are quite different from those of the God in whom we trust. In short, the world, together with Satan, is exerting influence in a variety of ways over our children, with the result that many of them are being drawn away from God and the Christian faith.

The prominent educational philosophy today encourages youngsters to create their own personal values rather than adopting those of their parents or a preexisting moral code like that in the Bible. Children are encouraged to decide for themselves what is right or wrong. Consequently, many youngsters end up living two lifestyles: one that fits in with their teachers and peers and one that pleases their parents at home. Children may be outwardly imitating their parents' Christian lifestyle, while inwardly believing in the world's philosophy. The dichotomy between these two conflicting philosophies eventually takes its toll. A clear spiritual battle continues to rage for our children's souls, no matter what age they are.

Encouragement for the Future
No matter how severe this battle, Christian parents can still be involved in influencing their children for Christ. After all, we trust in a God with whom "all things are possible" (Mt 19:26). Jesus' teaching in this regard is a huge encouragement when we recall not only what we have discussed already but also the following: our children are born with a bent toward sin; they are a complicated genetic mix of both their parents; and, maybe worst of all, they have had to endure imperfect parenting from imperfect parents.

Nothing, though, can prepare parents for the shock of finding out that their children will often exert their own independence as they grow up and make radically different decisions than their parents would make. Their loving and caring parents may not even begin to understand the reasoning behind many of these choices.

When a child's decisions are negative and hurtful, many parents fall into a state of despair. As they assess the past, the way they have brought up their children and the decisions they have made, they may conclude they were never cut out for parenting in the first place. They believe they have failed miserably at this most important of tasks. They may even wish now that they had never opted to have children at all.

Jim, whose story we considered earlier, fits this category. When Jody first stopped attending church, he coped with his pain because his three other children were still attending. Although Jim has a perfectionist streak, he could handle what he considered to be only a 25 percent failure rate. If you recall, what he could not cope with was the eventual rejection of God and the church by *all* of his children. That was just too much. He felt he had failed his wife, his children, God, and himself. While he put on a brave face, inside he was a broken man.

Normal Reactions

It is easy for us to sense that any or all of these emotional reactions to our children's decisions are wrong and to feel very bad about our disappointment, anger, hurt, frustration, and sense of guilt and failure. Yet Christians of all people should know that our Creator made us with emotions and feelings. We laugh, cry, get angry, or feel relaxed. Our moods change according to our circumstances. Furthermore, we cannot always control our emotions as we would like to.

If your feelings line up with any I have described, remember that it is inevitable to experience some emotional response to any life-changing decision a child of yours makes. This is not wrong, just perfectly normal.

Maybe because the issue we are discussing is a spiritual one and your child's rejection is of God and the church, you are particularly sensitive. To react to such a decision with deep and heartfelt feelings, however, is utterly natural. You must not allow yourself to be tormented any longer that there is something wrong with you. Almost certainly God feels at least as brokenhearted and upset as you do.

God Hurts Too

This brings us to consider from Scripture how God feels when people ignore him, rebel against him, or simply opt to live their lives as if he does not exist. The Bible is very open about God's response, and here we see the origin of the emotions that are features of the human personality, albeit now imperfect and tainted by sin.

When we start to read the Bible at the beginning, we turn only a page or two before we find God's sovereignty being challenged. Having created an amazing environment for humans to live in, God restricts Adam and Eve's lifestyle in just one way. When they ignore his prohibition and deliberately eat the fruit of the tree of the knowledge of good and evil, God has no alternative but to react. His curses, followed by his banishment of Adam and Eve from the Garden of Eden, were an expression of his sadness and anger over their rebellion. Sin has to be punished (see Gn 3:16-23).

Some generations later, when mankind's life on earth was epitomized by evil, God's response is graphically described. In Genesis 6:6 we are told that he "was grieved that he had made man on the earth, and his heart was filled with pain." Human depravity was such that God's perfect holiness was deeply offended wherever he looked on earth. Once again he could not stand by and let things continue as if this rebellion by his creation did not matter.

The Flood was God's method of expressing his anger, pain, and disappointment. Later he acted differently when he countered people's pride at the Tower of Babel by confusing the world's languages (see Gn 11:9), and in Abraham's day he destroyed the cities of Sodom and Gomorrah because their sin was "so grievous" (Gn 18:20). God cannot and does not ignore sin committed against him and his laws as if it does not matter.

Moses and the people of Israel learned this too. While Moses was on top of Mount Sinai receiving God's commandments for his people, the Israelites, under Aaron's leadership, made a golden calf and worshiped it. This incited God's anger (see Ex 32:10), and he sent a plague to strike the camp (see Ex 32:35). However, for all God's disappointment, he continued to provide and care for his people.

The Pain God Feels

Centuries later, in the era of Israel's history immediately preceding the Exile, God spoke eloquently through his prophet Hosea. Through him God revealed his ambivalent feelings toward rebellious and spiritually unresponsive Israel (see Hos 11:1-9). His frustration, pain, and hurt surface in verses 1-4, while his anger is obvious in verses 5-7. The conflict between these seemingly opposing emotions is highlighted in verses 8-9. Here we sense God's struggle to come to a clear-cut decision, but he does so by verse 9, where he announces his conclusion that his love and mercy must exert more influence than his desire to punish. You may find it helpful to study Hosea 11:1-9, noticing how God dealt with his own unresponsive children.

When the Bible describes God's anger, we need to understand that this is righteous anger. One example of this can be found in the Gospel of Matthew, when Jesus cleared traders from the temple courts in Jerusalem. Jesus explained that they were corrupting a sacred site which had been set apart for worshiping God (see Mt 21:12-13). A holy, pure, and morally perfect God cannot but react to sin that offends him to the core.

Maybe the most telling insight into God's response to sin and rebellion is found in the crucifixion of Jesus. Remember, Jesus had been present with the Father from eternity and had been actively involved in creation long before he became a man on earth (see Jn 1:1-4). The depth of love between Father and Son was the deepest the universe had ever known, yet on the cross Jesus knew that his Father had abandoned him (see Mt 27:46).

God has to react to sin—even when his own dear Son was left to bear it alone in indescribable agony on a cruel Roman cross. Words do not exist to convey the anguish felt within the Godhead that day as Jesus bore the sin of the world. To say God experienced suffering is the biggest understatement of all time.

God Comes Close

Maybe the revelation that God experiences hurt, frustration, disappointment, and anger (though not feelings of guilt and failure, of course) is enough to show you that your own feelings are legitimate. They are consistent with what it means to be a person. People naturally have feelings. They respond to what is going on around them, and they find that their emotions are especially provoked when things happen to them and to those they love and care about most.

God has feelings too. His emotions cause him to feel much the same as we do, especially when people step outside of his plan for their lives. When our children decide to live their lives independently of God, both he and we feel it inside. God knows their hearts and minds; he is aware of their decision, and he shares with us our reaction to it.

You will not regret it if you let God come close and share your pain with you today. His presence will be reassuring and strengthening. Remember that he has feelings as you do, so he empathizes with you over your children. To know that God is close at hand and that he fully understands can only help you.

However, while God is prepared to support us in our pain, he does not intend for us to remain locked into it for a long time. He has something better for us, but in order to find it, we first have to understand one of the ways God works on earth.

Two

God Will Help You to Understand His Plans

A worldwide American-based bank has just sent a letter offering me an "exciting new investment opportunity." First, though, they would like to talk with me about my future financial plans. Am I thinking of getting married, starting a family, buying a house, or preparing for retirement? In each case they say they can help me devise the perfect plan to ensure my financial security until I die.

To be honest, that letter is now in my wastebasket. I already have financial goals and a plan. I have other plans too—for our church, our family, holidays, writing, and the broadcasting work I do. From time to time, after careful thought and prayer, I write down what I believe to be God's way for my family and me to move forward. I always try to be creative and adventurous, while avoiding being unrealistic or irresponsible.

From eternity God has developed plans, too, and he has never been short of creative ideas. Evidence for this is apparent in everything good we find in our world and universe. After all, if the Creator had not conceived all these good things in his mind first and then put them in place, they would not exist at all. Christians know that the nature and character of the God in whom they believe and trust are demonstrated in what he has made and the way he has established life on earth.

God's Plan for Families

One of God's most creative concepts was that of families, and this was part of his plan for the human race from the very beginning. It was not the brainchild of a sociologist from a past generation. The idea of a mother, a father, and children sharing life together, with other members of the family nearby, was in God's mind long before it became a reality on earth.

What you and I have experienced of family life, as both children and parents, has probably not been ideal. This does not invalidate the concept as originally devised by God, however. Before time as we know it existed, God planned that parents should raise their children in a loving and secure environment. The children would then be able to learn about and prepare for their future as adults in what is often a painful and dangerous world.

It was also in God's plan that parents would pass on their faith to their children. This was not so that the children would have a hand-me-down faith in God but that they would get to know him as their own loving heavenly Father. God's clear desire was that every human being should grow up knowing and trusting him. Though human relationships with God were severely disrupted when Adam and Eve rebelled, God still remained very involved in the lives of the people he had made (see Gn 3:21; 4:6-7).

How God Works

This book is intended to provide practical help and encouragement for parents who desperately want to see their children come to faith in Christ, something God also desires. Before we can look at how we can work together with God to help this happen, though, we need to understand the way God operates and why this is so important. We are concerning ourselves here with an issue that is extremely close to the heart of God.

Although we may be oblivious to the fact, God is very much aware that Christianity could become grossly distorted on earth within a few generations. This can happen to any movement, philosophy, or religion—and often does. Some of these movements even become extinct. In centuries gone by, Christianity itself has come close to the edge of the precipice at various times. But God was careful when he planned his work on earth, and he provided special resources for believers.

First, there is the Holy Spirit, whose quiet and persuasive ministry in the hearts and lives of people affects them profoundly, whether they recognize it or not. We can see, for instance, how the Holy Spirit was at work in the early sixteenth century. He used Martin Luther and others as instruments to reform grossly unbiblical teachings of the medieval Roman Catholic Church, in which Luther was a priest. At that time Christianity was at a low ebb, but the "salvation by faith alone" message of the Reformation (led by Luther, Calvin, Zwingli, and others) and various movements within the Catholic Church itself enabled the Holy Spirit to protect God's investment in the world by rebuilding and expanding his church.

Second, God has provided his eternal truth preserved in the Scriptures. Here we find teaching about God, human beings, faith, salvation, forgiveness, heaven, and numerous key issues people need to know about if they are to enter into a meaningful relationship with God. Having both the Holy Spirit and the Bible, a man or woman can be a formidable spiritual influence in our dark world.

Parental Influence

God wants all believers to be spiritually dynamic, including parents. Parents have a unique opportunity to influence their offspring spiritually over many years, and God clearly desires that they should. After all, they have a special relationship within which to do so. On many of its pages, the Bible shows how God uses believing parents to help encourage faith in their children.

Ordinarily we identify a child's early years as the time when parents have the most effect on faith development. It appears, however, that Noah's faith may have had the greatest influence on his sons when they were grown men. Though there was not even a cloud in the sky, Noah followed God's instructions precisely, building an ark and taking his family aboard (see Gn 7:1).

If Noah's sons and their wives had not survived the flood, the human race would have been lost, both physically and spiritually. Noah's sons needed to know God for themselves so that the line of faith would continue after Noah's death. God's deep desire is to see many people of faith, people like Noah, emerge on earth in succeeding generations.

Jonathan is one of Noah's modern-day spiritual offspring. He lives in a small town with his wife and three children. He and Doreen have always sought to bring up their children to respect and trust God and have aimed to show them and teach them about God's love. They also brought up their children in a lively church that demonstrated the relevance of the Christian faith to life today. Recently Jonathan and Doreen were thrilled when their eldest daughter made her first public profession of faith in Jesus Christ. God wants parents to surround their children with loving Christians in this way, to encourage and teach the children to accept Christ for themselves.

Passing Faith On

God has always wanted living faith in him to be passed on. Abraham transmitted it to his son Isaac, then Isaac to Jacob, and Jacob to Joseph. While the Bible does not conceal the imperfections in some of these characters, it does reveal the way parents passed their faith in God on to their children. God's plan was that an unbroken chain of love and devotion to him should emanate from the families of the earth, being handed on from generation to generation.

The book of Exodus tells us that before young Moses went to live at Pharaoh's palace, he spent some time with his Levite parents, who undoubtedly taught him to believe in and trust God. Pharaoh's daughter had discovered Moses hidden in the bulrushes as a baby and then handed him back to his own family to be taken care of through his earliest years. Moses' faith developed fully when God entrusted him with the huge task of liberating the Israelites from slavery in Egypt. For many people the journey of faith begins during a childhood spent living with a godly family, as happened to Moses in his very early years.

It was that way for Samson too. Like other believing couples whose stories we read in the Bible, Samson's parents were unable to have children naturally. Only after God intervened, twice sending an angel to earth to tell them of his divine plans, did the woman conceive. Whatever the couple's quality of relationship with God was before that, there is no doubt that these encounters deepened their trust in him and gave them much more to share with their son spiritually as he grew up (see Jgs 13:2-25).

Faith Is Learned at Home

Surely the same thing also happened in Elkanah's home. One of his wives, Hannah, was unable to conceive. In distress one day, she pleaded with God to give her a son. He did, and we can only presume that Samuel, the youngster to whom God spoke so clearly while he was still a boy (see 1 Sm 3:2-10), and who became a wise and influential prophet, started his spiritual pilgrimage in the home where his life began.

These are not the only Old Testament characters whose first spiritual experience was gained in their childhood home. King David probably grew up in a godly environment (see 1 Sm 16:1-13), then later, having sinned, found God to be gracious and faithful (see Ps 51). Solomon, David's son, learned about faith from his father. Jeremiah also had this privilege because his father served as a Jewish priest (see Jer 1:1). Others whom God used to share their faith with their descendants include Ruth and Esther, and it was this commitment to encourage their younger relatives to trust God that preserved the Hebrew people through numerous disasters and persecutions.

When God was almost ready after centuries of preparation to send his Son to earth, we see the same thing happening again. Zechariah and Elizabeth were already committed to serving God long before a message from one of the Lord's angels changed their lives forever. The angel told them that God would give them a son through whom he would draw many of the Jewish people back to himself (see Lk 1:13-17).

When their son John the Baptist began public ministry some years later, he was clearly a man whose life was committed to God. Neither his message of repentance nor the way he proclaimed it (describing some of his hearers as "a brood of vipers" [Lk 3:7]) was likely to make him popular. Here was a man who had been encouraged by his parents to get to know God personally and was now faithfully declaring the word of God as he had been called to do.

Mary and Joseph are also among those taught by their families to be faithful to God. This is the only explanation as to why, when invited by one of God's angels to cooperate with God's plan to bring the long-promised Savior into the world, they agreed to take on this incredible task—that of parenting the Son of God on earth.

Investing in Young People

The apostle Paul recognized that Timothy had become a Christian through the godly influence of his mother and grandmother (see 2 Tm 1:5). When he realized he would have no physical children of his own, he adopted both Timothy (see 1 Tm 1:2) and John Mark as his spiritual sons. Paul knew that biological parents who are Christians are called by God to share their faith with their children, so he too needed to invest in young men who would continue to live the faith and share it with others when he could no longer do so.

Viewed humanly, it is because past generations of Christians have been faithful in passing on God's truth that you and I are believers today. What is more, my recent research shows that much of this communication has taken place in Christian homes. In other words, God's plan is still working.

To collect this information I surveyed 225 Christians at random during church services in both England and North America. This informal research revealed that 87 percent (195/30) of those who made up the congregations had been brought up in families where at least one parent exerted some Christian influence on the home. Of these people 77 percent (147/45) estimated on reflection that this had had at least a moderate impact upon their becoming Christians themselves.

Unobtrusive Witnessing

Also of interest is the fact that when asked at what age they first became Christians, 84 percent of the respondents indicated it was during their teenage years or before (53 percent of all respondents were twelve or under while 31 percent were teenagers). Interestingly, British research undertaken on behalf of *Churches Together in England* revealed that 70 percent of those who find faith do so by the age of twenty.[1]

It has been like this during the nineteen hundred years since the end of the biblical era. In that time great evangelists such as John Wesley, George Whitefield, and Billy Graham have been used mightily by God to win tens of thousands of people into God's kingdom as they have preached the gospel. Alongside this ministry, however, and usually taking place quietly and unobtrusively in homes across the world, has been the absorption of God's truth by hundreds of thousands of youngsters as they have grown up.

Among these was Anthony Ashley Cooper, later known as Lord Shaftesbury, the nineteenth-century British politician and social reformer. His strong Christian faith was jump-started in his home, but not by his parents in this case. When Shaftesbury was a young child, the family housekeeper, Maria Milles, used to put him to bed. A committed Christian, Maria sat him on her knee, taught him to pray, and told him stories from the Gospels, including those of the death and resurrection of Jesus. Shaftesbury first believed and became a Christian at that time, a decision that profoundly affected the rest of his life.[2]

Billy Graham, the world-renowned evangelistic preacher, was converted to Christ during a mission in North Carolina led by the Southern evangelist Mordecai Ham in 1934. Graham was sixteen at the time, and it was by no means his first exposure to Christianity. He had grown up in a family descended from Scots-Irish Presbyterians and had been taken to church every week from childhood.[3]

Plans to Win the World

These recollections show how God has been working out his plan through the centuries to win the world with his love. Thankfully, God can and does break into the lives of those whose parents have no belief in him at all. But God especially delights to accomplish his will on earth by working through generation after generation of the same family, as demonstrated by the detailed genealogy faithfully listed by Matthew (1:1-17).

Interestingly, I can glean two examples of this from my own family. The first is that I am a product of a believing family, although God had to work creatively to make it so. Neither of my parents was born into a Christian environment, but when my mother was a little girl, her parents sent her to Sunday school at the local Baptist church, although they did not attend themselves. My mother was converted and in her early twenties met my father there when a Christian friend with whom he worked brought him to the youth fellowship. By the time he and my mother married they were both believers, and I was born into a Christian family and grew up in the church.

Another branch of my family has perhaps a more fascinating story to tell. My great-granduncle James was converted as a young man in Brighton, a large town on the south coast of England. He served as a missionary in Brazil for thirteen years and founded *Help for Brazil* before becoming a pastor back in England. One of his sons, also named James, returned to Brazil and founded a Christian mission hospital in Anapolis, Goias State, living and working there until he died in his nineties.

Today his family continues to maintain and develop the work he pioneered. Dr. James Fanstone's two sons, Henry and

William, took over the hospital and its ministry before their father died, and now that they have semi-retired, entrusted responsibility to Dr. Henry's son, Dr. Billy, also an active and committed Christian. Under Billy's leadership, the work of *Hospital Evangelico Goiano* is as vibrant and valuable today as it ever was. In this case, not only has the faith of the father been passed to the son, but so has the vision for a specific work that God has called them to do.

God Draws People to Himself

In this chapter we have seen that God works in and through the lives of committed believing parents when he can. He desires to draw each of the offspring from every Christian family into a meaningful relationship with himself.

This happened in the lives of many biblical characters and has been continuing through the centuries since. Today God's plan is unchanged. It does not matter if you have children in your family aged 5, 15, 25, 35, 45, 55, 65, 75, or even older. If they are not enjoying a personal relationship with God, he wants to draw them to himself. What is more, he wants you to work in partnership with him to help it happen. Now let us see how it can.

Three

God Will Forgive and Heal Past Problems

"If only ..." Words uttered by us all from time to time. As we look back on our lives we identify so many things we would have done differently with the benefit of hindsight. *If only* I had made much more of my opportunity to study and learn as a teenager in school. *If only* I had not bought an old Volkswagen bus in the early 1970s without first having the chassis professionally checked for rust.

We all have to live with regrets, many of them substantially more serious than the two just cited. After all, in both cases, I was able to redress the problem with comparative ease. Though I left school with a pathetic academic record, I was able to study again and have since gained a college degree. After selling my disintegrating Volkswagen to a scrap merchant, I was able to buy another car and my mistake was soon forgotten.

By no means are all the "if onlys" in our lives so easily solved. I know people who now have a police or criminal record because of a hasty or poorly thought-out decision. Their records will stay with them for the rest of their lives, and they can do nothing to change that.

Sadly, the same thing can happen in marriage and family life. You may, like me, know a friend who became infatuated with someone other than his or her spouse. An affair followed, and the pain and hurt resulted in their marriage breaking down and eventually one of the partners seeking a divorce. It is sad, but it happens—and all the people involved carry the emotional scars for life, even if they do their best to conceal them.

In this chapter I want to help you review your track record as a parent. Until now we have assumed that most readers have brought up their children to be Christians. Other readers, however, may have become believers later in life and now want to see their adult children follow them into a personal relationship with God.

Imperfect Parenting

To begin with, we have to recognize and accept that the world has never witnessed a perfect human parent. Had Jesus had physical children we would have, but he did not. Even Mary and Joseph (with all due respect) were imperfect parents and made mistakes. The same is true of all of us who have been in the privileged position of having children in our care.

Parenting is undoubtedly one of the most difficult tasks on earth. It would be made much easier if children were born with most of their parents' strengths instead of, as it often seems, all of their parents' weaknesses. Most of us probably wonder at times if God arranges it deliberately to help further sanctify our character!

Author Sheila Bridge, in *The Art of Imperfect Parenting*, describes the dream most parents have:

> We'd all like to be a loving and lovable, wise and witty "ideal parent." Someone with the gentle wisdom of Bill Cosby, the dedication of Mother Teresa, the imagination of Steven Spielberg, all blended with a little honest simplicity and a pinch of humility. We may have set out on the adventure of parenting with that kind of ideal in mind, but it doesn't take long to discover that we do not need tuition [instruction] in how to be an imperfect parent; it comes to us quite naturally.[1]

An Inadequate Parental Role Model

This means that, as we look back over the years since our first child was born, each of us can think of numerous occasions when we blew it. What about the time when you completely lost your cool because your child refused point-blank to do his homework? Then there was the time when you were under pressure at work and swore at your spouse in front of the kids because the meal was not ready on time. We all have skeletons of one sort or another in our closets.

The worst thing in all of this was the impact that our indiscretions had on our children. They saw, listened, and took it all in. They might not have passed any comment, but they missed nothing. What their minds made of our exhibition we may never know. What we know for sure is that it left its mark.

This is what Susie feels as she reflects on life in her childhood home. Her parents were highly valued and respected members of their local church, but at home there was a high level of stress. This was due primarily, Susie felt, to her mother's tendency to nag and worry about relatively trivial issues. According to Susie, the atmosphere at home was quite different from the image her parents presented when together at church. There they somehow managed to ooze love and warmth, which made Susie uncomfortable, knowing the underlying stress and tension between them.

Now, just over a decade after leaving home at nineteen, Susie feels that she might have grown more spiritually if her mother had been a better Christian role model. She does not want to upset her mother by raising this issue with her, but nevertheless she feels the sadness quite deeply. Now it seems to her that the only person she can talk with regularly about this is God himself.

Making Bad Judgments

Then we can think of times when we have made bad judgments. Dennis tells of the time when his youngest son came into the house while he was watching a movie on TV. Robbie said that he was going to the park with some friends. He was only thirteen at the time, and it did not occur to Dennis that it was just getting dark. Dennis' mind stayed on the movie, and he simply nodded and grunted in Robbie's direction. An hour later when the movie ended, Dennis began to wonder where his son was.

Without his father knowing, Robbie had gone via the park to the nearby shopping mall. There he and three friends had dared one another to shoplift. The challenge was to see who could steal the most expensive merchandise. Dennis discovered what his son had been up to only when he received a phone call shortly afterward from a security guard in a software store. Robbie had been caught trying to steal computer games.

Dennis was shocked, embarrassed, angry, and feeling guilty for not even listening to what Robbie had said before he left home. He concluded that, had he probed a little more, he might have been able to stop this disastrous episode and spare the whole family a lot of pain. While he was angry with Robbie for stealing, he blamed himself even more for allowing it to happen.

Many Vices

Jeremy became a Christian when he was thirty-eight, and by then he had a sixteen-year-old daughter. He saw himself reflected in her in many unsettling ways. Her language was littered with swear words. She smoked, drank, and almost certainly slept with her boyfriend. She was probably on drugs, and she could be a formidable foe if she lost her temper. The longer Jeremy was a Christian, the more uneasy he was about the way his daughter was living her life.

He came to recognize, however, that Joanna was behaving in much the same way he and his wife had when they were in their mid-to-late teens. What is more, they had perpetuated this style of behavior for years once they started living together at seventeen. This stopped him from lambasting Joanna for her lifestyle, even though instinctively he wanted to.

After all, what other way of life had Joanna ever known? As a child she was taken to weekend rock concerts where sex and drugs were paraded openly. Violent fights between Jeremy and his common-law wife were frequent. While Jeremy desperately wanted to introduce Joanna to his new friend Jesus, he realized that through no fault of her own, she had been immersed since childhood in a very different lifestyle. Short of a miracle, she was not likely to change.

Much of Jeremy's pain was provoked by his guilt and grief over the fact that, of all people, he and his wife had introduced Joanna to the very things from which he now prayed desperately she would be freed. The closer he became to Jesus, the more this pain welled up inside him. Daily he prayed that God would somehow work a miracle in Joanna as he did when he burst in upon the life of Saul of Tarsus on the road to Damascus.

God answers a mother's prayers. Although it is too soon to know how Joanna will choose to live her life, we are aware that God answered the prayers of Monica, the mother of Augustine (A.D. 354-431). He became Bishop of Hippo and was one of the most influential leaders the Christian church has ever known. His childhood in Thagaste, North Africa, though, was hardly ideal. Augustine's father, Patrick, was a bad-tempered pagan reputedly often unfaithful to his wife. Augustine's mother, Monica, grew up with a liking for drink.

Monica's life changed after a servant rebuked her one day for being drunk. This reprimand "brought her to her senses and, under the conviction of sin, prepared her to receive the gospel. She became a devout Christian and soon became known for her godly living and faithfulness in prayer."[2] It was many years, however, before her son Augustine became a Christian.

Like many other teenagers, Augustine was unhappy about having to go to church and seemed to take more interest in the girls than the service! Later, while studying in Carthage, he met a servant girl, lived with her for thirteen years, and fathered a son. When he began to reflect seriously about ethics and religion, he initially rejected the Bible, and for ten years he followed the unorthodox Manichaean philosophy, which combined elements of Zoroastrianism, Christianity, and pagan religion.

Meanwhile Monica continued to pray for Augustine. Jesus Christ had dramatically changed her life, and she wanted her son to share the same experience. Augustine was feeling empty and dissatisfied with life when a friend persuaded him to go hear Ambrose, Bishop of Milan. Here he heard the truth and came to recognize how repugnant his life was in the sight of God. To his mother's delight, Augustine became a Christian when he was thirty-two and within a decade had been appointed Bishop of Hippo.

Monica died shortly afterward. However, she passed away knowing that despite the unhelpful influences she and her husband had exerted on Augustine during his childhood, God had heard her prayers and brought her son to himself. Of course, other parents cannot assume that the same will happen in their family, but the determined way in which Monica clung to God and his promises clearly provides an example for us to follow today.

Inadequate Christian Witness

At this point, perhaps, parents who are long-standing Christians need to face up to the kind of Christianity they portrayed at home while their children were growing up. Like it or not, there is only one approach to take here. You and I need to assess whether our children, by watching us and listening to us, received a truly biblical presentation of the Christian faith over the years.

Did they hear from their parents' lips that Jesus loves them?

Were they told that Jesus forgives us when we do wrong if we repent and ask him? Were they taken to church faithfully each Sunday by parents who displayed a determination not to miss worshiping God with others for almost any reason? Did their parents ever read the Bible to them at home and encourage them to do it for themselves?

As you now reflect on it, perhaps you can see that your children were given the impression that Christianity is harsh and legalistic, irrelevant, or of only mediocre importance. If so, then it is hardly any wonder that they have little time for the faith you supposedly hold dear. After all, they are only mirroring what they sensed was your true attitude to your faith. It may not have been what you said, but it certainly came through in what you did.

There is, of course, an opposite (and equally unhelpful) trap into which Christian parents—especially full-time Christian workers—can fall. This is when service rendered to God and others is obviously much more important to one or both parents than time spent with their children.

Second best. Danny was the son of a well-known minister whose city-center church drew a large congregation. Danny's obsession was soccer, and he loved to watch it and play it himself. His dad kept himself physically fit through regular jogging, yet he always seemed to be too busy to go to the park and kick the ball around with Danny.

Furthermore, Danny wanted so much to go watch his favorite team play, but as this was usually on Saturdays when his dad had to work, the only way he ever went was with a friend and his friend's dad. Danny always knew that it was second best. He wanted his own dad to be there with him.

Danny loved his dad deeply but could not help growing up with a grudge against God and the church. He felt it was grossly unfair that between them they deprived him of the time he needed with his dad doing the things he enjoyed best. Deep down he liked the church, and the people were always kind to him, but nonetheless, resentment started to grow as Danny got older.

It is so easy for well-meaning Christian parents to give a false and unhelpful image of Christianity to their kids. When Danny gets challenged with the message of the gospel sometime in the future, he will certainly find a barrier to it already in place. He will not deliberately balk at giving his life to Christ, but he and others who have seen an unhelpful and biased view of the Christian faith are less likely than some to be rushing to receive Jesus Christ as Savior and Lord.

Other Deterrents

By no means have we exhausted the list of factors that will make it harder for our youngsters to become Christians. As we discussed in chapter 1, the world is making a huge impact on impressionable young people today. Teachers who espouse a very different worldview and morality, political leaders who seem to have no concern for the need to tell the truth, the demoralizing effect of TV and movies—all play a major role in helping to shape the character of young people. None of this excuses a lack of personal integrity on their part, but it does mean that the Christian values their parents and the church ceaselessly try to instill are under constant attack.

Sadly, it was the critical and judgmental attitude of others that Katie saw in her own home that held her back for a long time from making a Christian commitment. Everyone at church thought her mother was so sweet. She always had a kind smile and was willing to help anyone in distress.

Katie, however, saw another side of her mother at home. The kind smile was much less apparent there, and her tongue could be vicious. Indeed, at mealtimes she would often criticize some of her church friends for being absent from church, for the clothes they wore, or for their failures with their children. Katie found her mother's two-faced approach very hard to reconcile with the faith she professed.

Of course, not all parents display all these tendencies, but it is probable that all display some. And it is likely that their more aware of their parents' deficiencies than the adults themselves, but when the truth hits the parents, it hits them hard. Any parent can have a difficult time coming to terms with what they have done and are doing that has made it harder for their children to commit their lives to Christ.

The Personal Consequences of Parental Inadequacies

What can these parents do? Sadly, none of us can turn back the clock. If we now see how our behavior fifteen or twenty years ago was spiritually detrimental to our youngster, who has since made it clear to us that she will never become a Christian, we can hardly ask if we can rerun that part of her life. Like every other human being on earth, we have to live with the consequences of our earlier mistakes.

What is hardest to handle, however, is that emotional baggage may still be very much alive long after the events causing it. While some people philosophically reckon that time is a great healer, others of us know that pain, hurt, anger, and resentment do not necessarily diminish just because a certain number of months or years has elapsed since an incident occurred.

Of the emotions that tend to stick around until they are dealt with, two are notoriously difficult to get rid of if your policy is to ignore them and pretend they are not there. Both anger and guilt have a dogged persistence about them, which means that, even if you think you have left a painful situation behind, they will continue to fester inside until you face them head-on and deal with the deep feelings you have probably buried.

Anger

As we saw in the first chapter, parents can quite easily become irritated with their children. They often realize upon reflection that they were merely cross at the rudeness, disobedience, or crude behavior they had witnessed. It was a short-term problem that quickly disappeared.

Anger is deeper than this. It takes us over; it plays with our minds; it may drive us to action; it will not go away. Some parents whose children have not come to faith are angry, and the anger tends to be directed in one or more of three ways.

Anger at their children. Some parents feel offended because their children have rejected the faith they were brought up in. Perhaps you as a parent can understand why. Sunday after Sunday, night after night during the week, you drove your children to the church so they could participate in youth activities. You watched, listened, prayed, encouraged, and invested everything you had in trying to help them find God. They never did.

Despite the fact that you love your children deeply and prob-ably have a great relationship with them today, under the sur-face you are offended by their rejection of your church and faith. You cannot understand it, and you do not grasp their rea-sons for it. The bottom line, however, is that you feel powerless to do much about it.

Anger at their church. Some parents insist for good reason that their children did not come to faith because the children's and youth ministry in their church was pathetically weak when they needed it to be vibrant and strong. This resulted in their chil-dren becoming convinced as they grew up that Christianity is utterly irrelevant and church totally boring. To be honest, no one can blame them. Faced with that evidence, many of us would have come to the same conclusion.

The fact that churches tend to go through cycles in their chil-dren's and youth ministry is hardly the point here, although it is often true. Sometimes parents have every reason to conclude that the church has let them down.

This complaint is not easy for a church to deal with. After all, a church is a body of individuals. It may have a leadership team, but unless one person has direct responsibility for youth work, there may be nowhere specific to lay the blame. Even if one per-son can be identified as the main culprit, it makes little sense to vent one's anger about deficiencies unless the problem has just occurred. Churches cannot put the clock back either.

Daniel's parents, Janet and Ted, are quite certain that their church, for all its seeming spirituality, flamboyance, and effi-ciency, has to accept responsibility for their son not coming to Christ as a teenager. The youth work was at a low ebb while

Daniel was in his mid-teens, and Daniel and the other three in his age group abandoned church in disgust just before his six-teenth birthday. He might have had a further opportunity to come to Christ had he not been tragically killed in a car accident a few months later.

Anger at themselves. Possibly the hardest type of anger to cope with is that directed inward. It can be very hard to identify, but when we see the consequences of our earlier behavior and actions, we feel sick on the one hand and wildly angry with our-selves on the other. Unless we confront that anger and deal with it, it will not go away.

What makes inner anger especially hard to deal with is that we find it difficult on our own to disentangle the anger inside us from other emotions. This is where we may need outside help. Our pastor, a counselor, or a psychiatrist may have to help us identify what we have bottled up over the years. Once the anger is uncovered and clear in our minds, we can start to deal with it.

Guilt

This is always hard to handle, too, and it is not made any easier by the fact that there is more than one type of guilt. June knows all about this. Now living alone, she is still trying to come to terms with the painful events of the past few years that culmi-nated in her leaving her husband. She can describe vividly the verbal abuse she suffered night after night as he came home intoxicated. He refused to admit that he had a problem, and in the end June knew that she would find peace only if she left him.

As a Christian, she was very reluctant to do this, and due to her feelings of shame, she stopped attending her home fellowship group, where she knew others had drawn close enough to her to notice that something was wrong. It took a long time before she eventually opened up to a counselor, who showed her that in reality comparatively little of what had gone wrong in her marriage was her fault. June had lived with unnecessary misery for many months. Her counselor explained that most of what she was feeling was false guilt.

False guilt is used regularly by Satan to impede the spiritual progress and effectiveness of Christians. God made us with a capacity to do right and wrong and to choose between them. He also placed a conscience in each of us, which, unless we dampen its voice and guidance, instinctively tells us the course of action that is morally right. In practice it tends to work the other way around, and we usually sense that one of the choices before us is morally dubious. If we want to live in a way that pleases God, we therefore know which option to avoid.

True guilt is quite different. It descends over us after we have committed a sin. It is specific (not a general feeling of worthlessness), and we know that God has been offended by what we did. What is even better is that God draws this to our attention, not to make us feel condemned and useless (as Satan does with his false guilt), but in order to provide us with an opportunity to repent and be forgiven. God is always looking for a positive opportunity to give us more of his grace.

God's Offer

It is not in God's nature to leave someone down when they could be standing on their feet. When he sent his Holy Spirit into the lives of Jesus' disciples at Pentecost about A.D. 28, it was so that his love and power could dynamically transform people's lives. God's tailor-made ministry to individuals on earth has gone on ever since.

The message we need to grasp concerns God's love and grace. Without demanding payment of any kind, God offers to help us in a number of different ways when we approach him humbly and acknowledge our need. A Christian parent suffering because his or her offspring has not yet come to faith can be an ideal candidate.

The specific ministry a parent in these circumstances can receive from God may be twofold.

Forgiveness

In one sense this book may have done you no favors thus far. Quite frankly, you might feel even worse than you did before you started reading. This may be because God has convicted you of sins and offenses you know you have never confessed and repented of. Deep down you know you must deal with these without delay.

How do we discover the peace that comes from knowing that God has forgiven us? We know that we have it once we have honestly and sincerely confessed our sin and repented of it. This cannot be done either lightly or superficially. God is more than willing to forgive, but he must know first that we find the sin we have committed as abhorrent as he does.

It is helpful to read the prayer of King David in Psalm 51, a prayer he uttered once he knew his secret affair with Bathsheba had been exposed. The psalm begins with David's plea for God to be merciful to him and is quickly followed by a heartfelt plea that God will wash away all his iniquity (see vv. 1-2). David has been made only too aware of the sin he has committed (see v. 3), and he recognizes that whatever the impact on himself and others, God has been more offended by his sin than anyone else has (see v. 4).

Being honest with God. If, having reviewed your life and especially your track record as a parent, you can see that your deficiencies may have hindered your children from coming to faith in Jesus, then you have a place at which to start praying to God. You do not have to pretend with him; you can simply pour out your regrets, making no attempt to justify what you did or why you did it. As David says in Psalm 51, "A broken and contrite heart, O God, you will not despise" (v. 17).

God is amazingly patient with us when we are honest with him. Because Jesus died on the cross to secure our pardon, God's mercy and grace flow freely to us when we truly confess and repent. In one sense there is nothing mysterious about this. As Hebrews 9:15 puts it, Christ "has died as a ransom to set them free from the sins committed under the first covenant." A legal transaction has taken place, and Jesus was punished severely for all our wrongdoing.

This is a most astounding miracle. It is stunning that God, who has been willfully rebelled against and ignored ever since he made people, should find this kind of compassion for us in his heart. If God acted in the way we often do, he would have abandoned or exterminated us long ago. The fact that he has not done so says vastly more about him and his love for us than it says about our own merits.

Metropolitan Anthony of Sourozh, the archbishop in charge of the Russian Orthodox Patriarchal Church in Great Britain and Ireland, reminds us of this when he describes the parable of the Pharisee and the Publican:

The Publican comes and stands at the rear of the church. He knows that he stands condemned; he knows that in terms of justice there is no hope for him. He is an outsider to the kingdom of God, the kingdom of righteousness and the kingdom of love, because he belongs neither to the realm of righteousness nor to the realm of love. But in the cruel, the violent, the ugly life he leads, he has learnt something of which the righteous Pharisee has no idea. He has learnt that in a world of competition, in a world of predatory animals, in a world of cruelty and heartlessness, the only hope one can have is an act of mercy, an act of compassion, a completely unexpected act which is rooted neither in duty nor in natural relationships, which will suspend the action of the cruel, violent, heartless world in which we live. All he knows, for instance, from being himself an extortioner, a moneylender, a thief, and so forth, is that there are moments when for no reason, because it is not part of the world's outlook, he will forgive a debt, because suddenly his heart has become mild and vulnerable; that on another occasion he may not get someone put into prison because a face will have reminded him of something or a voice has gone straight to his heart.

There is no logic in this. It is not part of the world's outlook, nor is it a way in which he normally behaves. It is something that breaks through, which is completely nonsensical, which he cannot resist; and he knows also, probably, how often he himself was saved from final catastrophe by this intrusion of the unexpected and the impossible, mercy, compassion, forgiveness. So he stands at the rear of the church, knowing that all the realm inside the church is a realm of righteousness and divine love to which he does not belong and into which he cannot enter. But he knows from experience also that the impossible does occur and that is why he says, "Have mercy, break the laws of righteousness, break the laws of religion, come down in mercy to us who have no right to be either forgiven or allowed in."[3]

God's grace and mercy to us are staggering. At a stroke you can be forgiven for the years and years when you failed to serve God in the way he wanted. Maybe throughout that time you were feeding your children negative impressions of Christianity. Yet once you see your fault, face it, accept it, and repent of it, God will forgive you in a moment.

God's generosity is an amazing thing. After all, he offers us not just cleansing now, but also the promise of his love in this life and the next. God's love will not stop at our death. The wonderful grace of God to undeserving human beings goes on forever and ever in eternity.

Receiving forgiveness. Where does this leave us? It leaves us forgiven by God and, hopefully, now able to forgive ourselves. This may not happen immediately. It may take time, as it did in Jennifer's life.

The way God burst into her life one day certainly took

Jennifer by surprise. She had gone to church as usual on a Sunday morning, knowing that for some time her spiritual life had been dull and uninspiring. She did not know why and had done little to figure it out.

Jennifer's pastor was away on this particular Sunday, and the visiting preacher was the minister of a neighboring church. As he talked about the cross, Jennifer suddenly saw in front of her a huge parcel of her unconfessed sin. In a flash she recognized that her attitudes, her priorities, her lifestyle, her life as Tom's wife, and her role as mother to Mandy and Jason were all terribly deficient. Before she went home, she repented of all this to God amidst plenty of tears.

The next day she still felt spiritually lethargic. This surprised her, and only later, as she chatted to a friend over coffee, did she realize she was angry with herself for what she had been like for so long, and angry that she had been too blind to recognize it. Bit by bit over the next few months, however, Jennifer faced herself in the mirror and gradually sorted it out. Now a very different person, she is receiving training to become a counselor.

A New Start

No one ever has been or ever will be better than God at helping people to begin again. The Bible makes this transparently clear. He is more than willing to help those who want to leave the past behind and start afresh.

The Bible states this truth clearly and categorically as it recalls the failures of some of its key characters but also describes how God used these people in spite of their sins. Abraham selfishly told lies in order to protect himself and his wife (see Gn 20: 1-13), yet God still kept his promise to him (see Gn 12:1-3).

Jacob tricked his brother out of receiving the blessing that should have been his (see Gn 27:1-29), yet God allowed him to have a stunning and spiritually unique dream (see Gn 28: 10-17). Saul of Tarsus was intent on persecuting and eliminating Christians (see Acts 8:3; 9:1-2), yet Jesus appeared to him in a life-changing vision (see Acts 9:3-9) that led him to become the most notable missionary and church planter the world has ever seen.

God will always give a second chance to those who want to work in partnership with him. Maybe your children have grown up and left home by now, but this does not mean that God cannot and will not use you to reach them for him. The opportunity you had to influence them for him when they were in your primary care has gone, but this does not mean it is too late for God to use you. Remember that it is never too late as long as they remain alive on earth.

Changed from the inside. Mary was so glad to learn this. She became a Christian just as her last child was finishing high school and preparing to go to college. For years she had presented her children with her cynical agnosticism. They were now well indoctrinated by this and highly unlikely ever to be open to Christianity. The damage had been done.

Then, through meeting a Christian at work, Mary found her attitude softening and within months became a Christian. For a long while she looked back with deep regret at the damage she had done to her children. She knew that of all people they were far less likely than most ever to share her faith in Jesus. She wished she could take them back to their childhood again and do it all differently.

At a women's Bible study at a friend's house one lunchtime, God chose to show Mary that she could still influence her children. As the women studied the life of Moses, Mary saw that if she devoted herself to spending time in God's presence, as Moses had, her face could shine with the glory of God (Ex 34:29).

She rededicated herself to God that day, and she left her friend's house knowing she would now start telling her children the story of what God had done to change her life. An upcoming birthday celebration, which would bring the whole family together for a weekend, would provide just the occasion.

Moving On

Mary was able to move on in her faith when she finally stopped regretting the past and allowed God to work in the present. In the same way that an athlete cannot hope to compete if he is still nursing a past injury, so Christians cannot serve God effectively in the present if problems from the past still dog their steps.

Thankfully, Christians can be forgiven and healed through the grace of God. If you have not yet allowed God the freedom to get rid of the excess baggage in your life that continually weighs you down, why not do it now? Then we can move on to see how your life can still be used by God to make a positive spiritual impact on your children.

Four

God Will Work Through You As You Persistently Pray

Now we come to the really important issue of how God could start to affect and penetrate the lives of your children, whatever age they are. This is inevitably where the going gets tough. After all, your offspring seem to have come to some kind of conclusion about Jesus already, even if you consider it to be based on wrong information.

We may as well face reality: once your children have made a decision to reject the Christian faith, it will be hard for them to change their minds. Perhaps your children grew up in a Christian home and you took them to Sunday school and church until, in their teen years, they thought it was boring and irrelevant and gave up on it. Many years may have elapsed since then, but they seem to have no intention or desire to change their minds.

Alternatively, perhaps you came to faith when your children were already grown-up, and the only Christian influence they have experienced has come from you since you were saved. In this case your children are probably largely ignorant about Christianity and may consider you weird for having become religious.

Either way, there seems little chance that your children and any family they now have around them will become believers. Statistics tell us that the majority of Christians first come to faith in Christ before they cease to be teenagers.[1] Does this suggest that it is now far too late to expect your family to do a spiritual about-face?

If you seriously thought that, I doubt you would be reading this book! It is one thing, however, to consider vaguely what it might take to see your children's lives transformed by God and quite another to believe that it could happen. According to God's Word, it could!

Handle With Care

Let us clarify this by recognizing that you are not going to achieve this change of heart in your children on your own. As we have observed already, there was a time when you were able to dominate your children's way of thinking and acting. When they were preschool age, you made the majority of their decisions for them. You did so in order to teach and train them, preparing them for their future independent lives.

As time went by and your children grew up, you had to get used to the fact that they were making more and more decisions on their own. They chose with whom they wanted to play, what they wanted to watch on TV, and where they would go for their birthday party treat. Later they decided in which academic subjects to major at school, whom to date, and what career to pursue. Not all of these decisions were theirs alone, but they developed an independence from the parental control that earlier had been normal and right.

That this transition from childhood to adulthood has already taken place means that you cannot exert more than a very limited influence on them now. For you to try would be unwise and might well be construed as interference. As parents we have to recognize that we will never be able to push or even nudge our children and their family into God's kingdom, however much we want to. This is not the way to achieve our desire; we need to find another.

There is a better path, a path that will accomplish God's work far more effectively than our efforts to do it alone. Just imagine what we would be like if, on our own, we could get people saved! We would not really need God, and we would become unbearably arrogant. God will never allow such a poor scheme to flourish.

God's Unique Way

His way is almost the complete opposite of ours. It is hugely different in that it puts all the responsibility for saving people onto God himself. I say it is "almost" completely opposite because God does not always work in isolation. More often than not, as he works on earth he seems to look for at least one, and often many, partners. Amazingly, and despite the fact that he has hosts of angels he could call upon, God's partners are invariably human beings like you and me.

The way in which he collaborates with us varies enormously. Often he involves us in practical ways. Something we say or the way we respond will provoke a response in someone who is listening or watching. As they mull over what they have heard or seen, they become open to the gentle but penetrating work of the Holy Spirit. Gradually they find themselves being drawn closer to God—or at least challenged to trust him.

Jane, a social worker, was asked by her manager to establish in her local community some counseling centers that would be staffed primarily by trained volunteers. Each would operate as a drop-in center so that local residents would have somewhere to turn when faced with anxiety or a crisis.

Aware that churches could make ideal centers, Jane built relationships over the next few months with a number of Christians and churches. As she did so, she found herself being deeply affected by what she saw and experienced. Gradually she was drawn toward Jesus Christ, whom these people loved, honored, and sought to serve. Eventually she made her own personal commitment to Christ.

A few months after she was baptized as a believer, Jane heard from some friends at church that a woman had been praying for her for months—in fact, since they had first met. The woman who quietly and faithfully prayed in the background provides an example for us of how God works. He encourages us to believe in something that clearly he *could* do, although at the time there is probably not the slightest evidence that he *will* do it. We are simply to pray in faith, trusting him for the result.

An Amazing Partnership

It is at this point that this wonderful partnership is created. We have so little to offer except simple trust in the living God, and even that depends on his giving us the gift of faith before we can exercise it. In amazing love and grace, he opts to invest resources in a given situation or person in response to the trust that is placed in him.

This is incredible to say the least, but it is precisely what Jesus taught his disciples (see Mt 17:20-21). After all, it is not as if there is any equality in this partnership. Far from it! On the one hand we have the almighty, eternal, all-loving, and ever-faithful God, while on the other there are Christian human beings. Their hearts may be dedicated to God, but they fail constantly to live up to both his and their own expectations. When God's will is not done on earth, it is always the human element that has failed to deliver.

Let us clarify the purpose of this chapter. It is not intended to explain why prayer is important or the impact it can make. Rather, it takes for granted that you know this already and that you often pray and trust in God's fatherly care. It assumes that you recognize his infinite power and regularly commend to him those you care about who have not yet come to faith in Jesus Christ.

The plan here is to explore in Scripture the *partnership* that can develop between God and his people as they pray and trust him to answer. Naturally, we will relate this to God's call to you to pray for your children so that, even as you read these pages, your faith in God's ability to work in their lives will grow.

The Cooperative Believer

Let us begin with a man whose story is told in the book of Genesis and for whom I have a great deal of respect. We know little about Noah's background. We are told that when he was five hundred years old, "he became the father of Shem, Ham, and Japheth" (Gn 5:32). We also learn that he found "favor in the eyes of the Lord" (Gn 6:8) because he was "a righteous man, blameless among the people of his time, and he walked with God" (Gn 6:9). This last clause—"he walked with God"—suggests a rich, in-depth relationship between God and Noah.

When God became grieved and distressed by the evil that was corrupting the world, he made a clear-cut decision. "I will wipe mankind, whom I have created, from the face of the earth," he said (Gn 6:6-7). Even as he was speaking, however, he knew he had to make an exception. After he assessed the life of Noah, God knew he could not condemn him and his family in the same way he had everyone else. This would be a gross injustice.

To spare Noah and his close family from the extermination that would befall the rest of the human race as the rains fell, God needed Noah's cooperation. They would have to work as partners from this point on. Noah and his family needed a ship that would float on the impending flood waters, and it had to be built to God's specifications.

Of course, God was perfectly able to build such a vessel himself; it was well within his capability as Creator of the universe. So it was not God's inability to build the ark himself that prompted him to select Noah as his partner—*it was his desire to enrich Noah's life as he learned to trust God more.*

An Emerging Relationship

Exactly how their relationship developed is hard to tell from the Scriptures. In Genesis 6–9 we find a great deal that God said to Noah, but the only recorded words of Noah come from a time long after the Flood when Noah felt offended by the action of his youngest son (see Gn 9:25-27). Yet we do know from Genesis that "Noah did everything just as God commanded him" (6:22).

Noah's response was to obey God's detailed instructions precisely. He was a man who as a matter of course daily "walked with God" (Gn 6:9), in complete contrast to the degenerate society around him. Noah talked to God and listened to him. Over the years he had learned to recognize God's voice and had come to trust completely what God shared with him.

As he and God already had a close bond, Noah knew there was only one thing to do when the Almighty burst into his life with news of an impending global disaster. He must have felt both privileged and relieved that God was giving him and those closest to him a means of being saved. Without delay he started gathering the materials needed to build the ark. He understood that when God points out which path to take, a person must get up and start walking.

Peter and his wife, Johnnie, knew the path they should take when an early-morning call informed them that their twenty-year-old son, Richard, was in jail, charged with narcotics possession. Earlier, knowing that Richard had developed a drug habit, they had told him that if he continued to use drugs and ended up in prison, they would not bail him out.

Later that same day they visited him and stuck by their word. They told Richard clearly and precisely of their love for him and of their willingness to help if and when he was ready to change, but they left him in custody and drove home. They had no doubt that this was what God wanted them to do and that ultimately he would take care of the situation.[2] Peter and Johnnie were people who prayed regularly, obeyed God, and then left the results to him.

More than anything, God looks for his partners to cooperate fully with him and to obey without questioning. This was not easy for Noah, who no doubt attracted great ridicule from his neighbors. Nor was it easy for Peter and Johnnie, who found themselves deeply torn as they left their son Richard in jail. They say they had "a quiet confidence that God was in control," just as Noah did while he was building the ark to the precise specifications God had given him.

Acting in Obedience

As you pray for your children, God will be working toward developing a partnership with you. This means that there may be times when he asks you not only to continue to pray but also to act in accordance with what he guides you to do. Your cooperation is likely to make a substantial difference in how effectively God can work within your family.

Jenny and Roland had both been sent to Sunday school when they were children. At that time they lived in different parts of the country. Interestingly, both gave up attending church in their teens, although because of a vibrant youth group he attended, Roland had stayed in church slightly longer than Jenny. By the time they married and had children of their own, neither of them considered the Christian faith at all relevant to them.

Only after their children had grown up and left home did Jenny and Roland become friends with their new next-door neighbors. Pam and Gerry were committed Christians, and as the friendship between the two couples developed, Jenny and Roland found themselves admiring Pam and Gerry's attitudes, serenity, and approach to life. It took almost five years before Jennie and Roland were ready to make a Christian commitment of their own, but just before they both celebrated their sixtieth birthdays, they each entered into a personal relationship with Jesus.

At first their three children thought this was funny. Although they had always had a deep respect for their mom and dad, they gently ridiculed their parents' newfound faith and the church-going that resulted from it. Jenny and Roland took it all in their stride but wanted James, Ruth, and Brian to become Christians too.

Being Sensitive

Gradually this couple came to realize that it might take at least as long for their children to come to faith as it had taken them. In time they reluctantly agreed they must act sensitively. They committed themselves to pray daily for each of their now grown-up children but decided they would speak to them directly about the gospel only when their children raised the subject first.

Their patience was rewarded when, as they washed up after lunch the next Christmas Day, their daughter Ruth remarked that Christmas must now have a new significance for them. Long before this day, Jenny had promised God she would coop-erate with him whenever he gave her the opportunity, so she sprang into action and shared simply but honestly with her daughter what knowing Jesus meant to her.

Ruth is still a long way from making a Christian commitment of her own, but that ten minutes of discussion in the kitchen was the highlight of Jenny's Christmas. She now tells God regularly that she is ready and willing to do anything he asks of her so that others, and especially her children, can discover Jesus in their own lives.

The Trusting Believer

As with the rest of his partners whose stories are told in Scripture, God chose Abram from among many other people. Unlike Noah's story, we are not given a description of Abram's faith at the outset, but as we follow his life, we find him to be a man who both listened to and talked with God. Furthermore, when he understood divine directives that were personal, he "believed the Lord, and he credited it to him as righteousness" (Gn 15:6). There was a close bond between the Almighty and his servant Abram.

One way in which God challenged Abram to demonstrate the depth of his faith was calling him to relocate from Haran to Canaan: "Leave your country, your people and your father's household and go to the land I will show you" (Gn 12:1). The letter to the Hebrews adds that Abram "obeyed and went, even though he did not know where he was going" (11:8).

Such action springs from a relationship built on very deep trust. Indeed, if Abram had gone for any other reason, he could be described as reckless and foolish. However, during many earlier years he had developed a rock-solid relationship with his unseen God and Lord, and there was now no question in his mind about God's care for him. Because this was the case, we know Abram's response was a step of faith and courage.

As Abram had allowed God to play an increasingly important part in his life, he had found the Almighty to be wholly trustworthy. The level of his faith had gradually grown over the years as he had shared his needs with God and they were met and as he had voiced his doubts and fears to God and was reassured by him. The result was that, when God asked a big thing of him (to relocate), he was prepared and willing to do it.

A Growing Faith

As we devote ourselves to building an ever-deepening relationship with God through prayer, we too will find that our faith gets stronger. Bit by bit we will find that we expect God to do bigger and greater things. The more we pray, the more we will anticipate by faith what God will do in response to our simple but heartfelt prayers. As with Abram, leaving for an unknown destination, it is all about trust.

Karen is a good example of a wife and mother who is developing a deep trust in the God whom she knows has revolutionized her life. Converted in her teens, Karen married a Christian man, and together they brought up their children in a stable Christian environment. Karen felt both desperately sad and helpless when, one by one, their children turned their backs on God and their family's church. It was while she was sitting in church one Sunday that God spoke to Karen clearly and precisely about what he was calling her to do.

Jeff, her pastor, was explaining in detail the meaning of faith from Hebrews 11:1. He said that faith exists only when you have no evidence whatsoever that anything will result from your simple trust in God, and that the moment you have proof, it ceases to be faith. All through the sermon Karen kept thinking about her children and their need of Jesus, even though they could not see it. Before she left church that morning she told God she would trust him to bring each of her children to himself before he took her to heaven.

Four years have passed, and Karen is still praying regularly for her children. Nothing much seems to have changed in their lives since she began, but a lot has changed in her. If you were to ask her today about her level of faith, Karen would tell you how she is absolutely certain that God will honor the faith she is placing daily in him. Maybe God's call to you is similar to his call to Karen.

The Adaptable Believer

Peter, Jesus' disciple, had failed Jesus by publicly denying him on three distinct occasions, and he felt extremely guilty. Even though he had been let down by Peter, Jesus still loved and valued him as his friend. He ministered personally to Peter in Galilee, making it clear that he wanted Peter to play a continuing part in his future plans. Not long after being reinstated by Jesus as a disciple, Peter came to the point in his life where the whole of his three years' training must have seemed extremely relevant and worthwhile.

Peter's relationship with Jesus was based on a lively communication between them. During Jesus' earthly ministry Peter was in the privileged position of not having to pray to him; he just met and talked with his master face to face. However, in the time that Jesus spent with them, he taught Peter and his friends to pray—something that would be a vital means of communicating with Jesus after he was no longer with them physically. Clearly, Peter and the other believers made a habit of praying regularly once Jesus had left them and ascended into heaven (see Acts 1:14; cf. 3:1).

Peter knew from Jesus' promise that not long afterward the Holy Spirit would come (see Acts 1:4-5). What he did not know is what would happen after that. This was the point at which the preparation and training Peter had received from Jesus suddenly made sense. Once the Holy Spirit had come and Peter and 120 other believers had flooded on to the streets to share the Good News, a problem arose. Some bystanders suggested that the commotion was attributable to the kind of spirit that normally comes in a bottle. Somebody had to counteract this and explain the true circumstances—quickly!

Taking a Lead

Peter then suffered a spine-chilling moment. It dawned on him that since Jesus had nicknamed him "the rock," the others would look to him to take a strong lead. Was he ready for it? No. Had he prepared himself? No way. Did he feel up to the task? Definitely not. There is little doubt that Peter was terrified at the prospect of having to represent his departed master in front of all these people who had totally misunderstood the events that had taken place.

When Peter had climbed out of bed that morning, he had had no idea this was the day on which God had chosen to fill him with the Holy Spirit. He did not even know what that really meant. Now, as an ordinary working-class fisherman from Galilee, he found himself faced with the challenge of making his first big-time public address.

He had probably felt moderately comfortable sharing the Good News of Jesus a few minutes before with a small group, even though he had found himself doing so in a language he had never learned. He had understood the gist of what he was saying, but the words that came out of his mouth were not intelligible to him. But the amazing thing was that the people to whom he was speaking seemed to understand them totally. Furthermore, they were actively interested in what they heard. Now, though, Peter was being asked to do something completely different—and infinitely more demanding.

The Example of Jesus

Maybe his mind went back to what his master and teacher, Jesus of Nazareth, had had to face during his three years of ministry. Sometimes unexpected things happened to Jesus. For example, on the way to Jairus' house, a needy woman in the crowd believed that all she had to do to receive healing was to touch his robe. Even though he was on his way to help Jairus' family, Jesus stopped to heal the woman (see Mk 5:21-43).

Maybe Peter also recalled what happened when he, James, and John returned with Jesus after their master's transfiguration. After all the spiritual stimulation and uplift of that occasion, they found themselves thrust into a situation where the rest of Jesus' disciples were being harassed for their inability to free a boy from an evil spirit. Without hesitation, Jesus liberated the boy by a release of divine power (see Mk 9:2-29).

Jesus was never perturbed by these interruptions and responded quickly to any necessary change of direction. Mind you, he did so while maintaining what seems to have been a regular prayer session with his heavenly Father (see Lk 4:32; 5:16; 6:12; 9:18). This was clearly where Jesus received a fresh infilling of spiritual power.

Now, after praying with his friends, Peter had the opportunity to stand up for his master—but in a very different way from anything he had ever done before. Maybe he had done some fairly low-key preaching while out training during Jesus' ministry (see Lk 9:1-6), but that was nothing like this. Standing there, as some in the crowd made fun of him and his friends, Peter must have felt apprehensive, but he knew what he had to do.

Using God's Resources

Peter had to defend a unique act of God to an excited and animated crowd. He knew he had just been touched directly by God as the Holy Spirit had filled his life. He also knew that his master, filled with the same Holy Spirit, had never exhausted God's spiritual resources when faced with unexpected situations in the past. Therefore, as Peter stood up and began to speak, he trusted that the same would be true for him too. It was, and the result was three thousand new Christians that day.

Gillian and Roger were very open with each other about how tough they were finding it to cope with their family situation. Their son Martin had been brought up in a Christian setting and taken to church since he was born. He was dedicated in the church and went through Sunday school, but at the age of fifteen he decided he had had enough of church and gradually drifted away. By his sixteenth birthday he had left the church for good and had no intention of returning.

Two years later he moved out of the family home, and it was a mere twelve months after this that his parents were horrified to discover he had become hooked on drugs and was living in a commune that believed in free sex within the community. Until then Gillian and Roger had kept praying for Martin. Now they were so horrified and embarrassed at their son's situation that they seriously considered disowning him. In their view he had deliberately chosen to rebel against everything they stood for and believed in.

How God Responds

Only two weeks after that, while still trying to come to terms with their son's choices, Gillian and Roger were studying the Bible in their weeknight home fellowship group when Frank, one of the other people present, shared his testimony. He described a particularly rebellious phase in his early life and attributed his return to God and the church to the continuing love and prayers of his godly parents and God's answering them. Frank knew nothing about Martin, but on hearing Frank's testimony, Gillian and Roger sensed that God was calling them to reconsider their attitude toward their son.

Due to their respective upbringings, neither Gillian nor Roger found it easy to forgive others, and for a grueling twenty-four hours, they discussed and prayed about what they should do. They eventually sat down and wrote a letter to Martin that promised him their love and prayers *whatever* he did in and with his life. They were careful not to condone his lifestyle but reinforced his status as their son, promising always to be there for him if he decided to change his way of life and come home.

Prayer, accompanied by a willingness to act in new ways as God's Spirit leads, is another of the marks of the cooperative believer. Partnership with God requires us to be adaptable.

Knowing How to Pray

It is one thing, however, to know that we can and should pray but quite another to do so in a way that is relevant. While of course our chief concern is to pray for our children's salvation, this is not the only request we can bring to God on their behalf. He is as concerned as we are about the numerous everyday matters in their lives.

With this in mind, we can pray about their health, safety, financial stability, and any number of issues relating to their employment, vacations, and way of life. Seeing answers to prayer in even simple things can help to build our faith and show us that God is at work in our children's lives, even if they have not yet come to faith in Christ.

Furthermore, if our children know that we are praying about their specific needs and then those needs are supplied, it may help them better understand the care and concern that God has for them.

God Is Looking for Partners

Whatever your family situation, God wants to be involved in helping your children come to faith. He has huge resources at his disposal and is more than willing to share them. He does this when he sees the followers of Jesus taking their faith seriously, asking for his help and believing he will answer. God is looking for praying partners with whom and through whom to work as his Holy Spirit is released.

Often in the teaching of Jesus we find him promising that our Father in heaven will hear every sincere and genuine prayer (see, e.g., Mt 7:7-8). More than this, he encourages persistent prayer (see Lk 11:5-8), making it plain, for example, that God will not get tired of our continually asking him to work in the lives of our children. Without a doubt, God is seeking out those who are truly hungry and thirsty for him, to transform their situations so that he can be glorified.

The way God has worked in the life of musician Richard Jon Smith demonstrates how remarkably he answers prayer. Richard grew up in Cape Town and was baptized and confirmed in the Dutch Reformed Church of South Africa. However, he rejected the church during his teenage years. He says, "I really stopped going to church at about the age of sixteen because I started falling asleep in the services! I was getting drawn into the secular world, and I wanted nothing else other than to be a singer and write songs and earn a lot of money."

After years of touring as a musician, he got the break he had hoped for—a song that rose to number one in South Africa and stayed there for nine weeks, making him a household name. More success followed, but then he moved to England and gained a lot of experience as a record producer. He still recalls his excitement at being asked to produce some of the music for the *Jewel of the Nile* film soundtrack.

Meanwhile, back in Cape Town, Richard's mother continued praying for her son, but it was only when Richard and his wife were on a trip to America in 1995 that they came back to God.

"My mum is still active in the church and she is eighty-two years old," he reports. "I truly believe her prayers have helped me over the years. You know, when a mother prays for a child, I don't believe there is anything stronger. The Lord listens, and she has been very obedient. It's been an important part of my life because I know that no matter where I am, whatever I am doing, my mother is praying for me."[3] Recently he has released his first Christian praise and worship album.

God is looking for praying people who, like Richard's mother, will stay close to him. Besides this, he wants his partners to be cooperative, trusting, and adaptable so that he can work in and through them to change not only the situation about which they pray, but also to change them as people.

As we move on to explore how God can shine through you to your children, we must not only ensure that we have understood the need to pray for them with sincerity and persistence but have started to *do* it. It is so easy for us to talk about prayer and agree that it is important; it is much harder to commit ourselves to doing so regularly. Yet, if we want to see God work in our children's lives, this is what we must do. It is where our partnership with God begins.

Five

God Will Shine Through Your Witness

When reading the Bible, we are never left in any doubt that it is God's desire to draw every human being on earth into a relationship with himself. In the Old Testament era, his chosen agent was the Jewish nation. Now that Jesus his Son has died, risen, ascended, and sent the Holy Spirit, it is his church. In order to keep working in and through his people on earth, the three key things that God continually calls his people to do are to worship, pray, and witness.

Scripture reveals to us that God is determined to communicate with humankind. Such communication was easy and natural until Adam and Eve sinned. Then it became more difficult because the human race was always more likely to choose any option that would best suit its rebellious and selfish nature.

When God called Abram into his service, he wanted to use this man and his descendants so that "all peoples on earth will be blessed" (Gn 12:3). Centuries later, and in fierce opposition to the Jews' exclusive view of their uniqueness, the Lord declared that his house would be called "a house of prayer for all nations" (Is 56:7). Jesus later reinforced this declaration. After his earthly work was virtually completed, he told his friends to "make disciples of all nations" (Mt 28:19). God wants every person living in every age to enter into a loving relationship with him.

This is easy to say but hard to implement. How can such a huge goal ever be accomplished? Jesus gave us the answer just before he returned to heaven. As his followers became his "witnesses" throughout the world (Acts 1:8), they would communicate God's love for each individual from person to person. The theory is simple. Sadly, the practice has rarely worked as God intended, due to human frailty and sin.

There is, though, one setting in which you might think it would be comparatively easy to communicate God's love. When a human family includes one or more Christians, surely the Christian faith can be shared in such a way that others decide to become members of God's family too. As we saw in chapter 2, this is an important part of the divine plan.

While it is relatively simple for parents to share their faith with young children, it is more difficult when their offspring are older and may have left home. How can committed and dedicated Christian parents help their now grown-up children meet Jesus personally?

Let us look at three important ways you can influence your children for God.

Be Accessible for God to Use As His Instrument

Many believers attend worship and go to other Christian meetings but stay in the background, allowing others whom they consider to be more gifted to do the majority of the work in the church. They believe that to be used by God a person needs to have certain dynamic qualities and spiritual gifts. They assume that the people God uses most tend to have big personalities and the capacity to charm and enthrall their congregations. While they may admire such people, they know they personally are not like that at all. Believers who make this assumption are often quiet people who feel very ordinary.

Maureen is like this. Born the youngest in a large family, she grew up feeling a bit like a spare part. She proved herself academically at a university, where she also became a Christian. After leaving the university, she got a good job. She was quiet and shy, though, both at work and within her church. She felt she had little to offer apart from the skills she was specifically trained in. It took some months of private Bible study with her pastor to show her that God had gifted her in many more ways than she had previously thought.

Maureen is not the first person to feel unsuited for God's work. Moses was quite certain God had picked the wrong man and told him so (see Ex 3:11; 4:13), while Jeremiah felt that his age ruled him out of contention (see Jer 1:6). That both these men are recognized today as having been godly and spiritual shows that God is capable of taking people who feel ill-equipped and inexperienced and using them to accomplish his plans.

As we saw in the last chapter, God is looking for partners so that ordinary human beings can collaborate with him in his desire to reach the world with his love. As those who have had their own lives changed by him, God intends that they should be open, accessible, and available to him. When they are, his love, grace, and the message of Jesus can flow through them.

What characteristics do such people need to have? The Bible tells us clearly.

Holiness

Because God is morally pure and perfect, disobedience and rebellion offend him deeply. Such disobedience is called sin. Typical of God's response to sin was his reaction to Adam and Eve when they blatantly defied his instructions about a particular tree in the Garden of Eden. He cursed them and banished them from his paradise because he found their attitude and behavior so offensive (see Gn 3:16-19).

God's view of sin was also demonstrated when the prophet Nathan confronted King David after the king had committed adultery with another man's wife, then ordered the husband to the front lines in battle, virtually assuring his death (see 2 Sm 12:1-10). God's message through Nathan was clear: the Almighty was angry. He had given David so much, yet the king had abused his God-given freedom and manipulated a situation for his own pleasure and gain.

Mercifully, God provided his Jewish people with a means to find forgiveness for their sins. As they presented sacrifices to God, he forgave their wrongdoing. His mercy and forgiveness allowed the people to approach him again because only those with "clean hands and a pure heart" can approach God (Ps 24:4). Almighty God cannot and will not allow himself to come into contact with sin.

Purity in relationships. Mary knows how truly God wants us to live pure lives. While happily married now, she knows how perilously close her marriage came to collapse when she had an affair with a colleague at her office. Her youngest child had just started school when Mary returned to work and quickly found herself admiring a man who worked in the next room. Like her, he was a Christian, although he had not been one for long.

As time passed, Mary found it increasingly difficult to control her thoughts and feelings about Chris. He seemed to like her too and one day invited her to go to a bar for a drink with him before going home. In less than a month they had rented a motel room, telling their spouses they had to work late.

Mary broke off the relationship soon after this, unable to regain the inner peace she had enjoyed before as a gift from God. She knew that she had sinned deeply against God, and against her husband, children, parents, and church as well. Only in the confidential setting of a counselor's office did she rediscover God's love, following a tearful time of repentance before him.

Purity in thoughts and motives. God is not only concerned about sexual purity, however. Jesus' teaching in the Sermon on the Mount shows that God views our thoughts and motives as being as important as what we actually do and say (see Mt 5: 21-48). The story of Ananias and Sapphira in the book of Acts is a dramatic demonstration of the importance God places on our attitudes as well as our actions. Because this couple lied to the apostles, giving only a portion of their money while declaring that they had given it all, they both died on the spot. Their moral failure before God was due to their mutual agreement to deceive the Jerusalem church. In so doing, they had actually lied to the Holy Spirit (see Acts 5:1-11).

Living God's way. In his letter to the Philippian believers, the apostle Paul sums up the way Christians should live. He says that not only should they recognize what is true, noble, right, pure, lovely, and admirable, but they should also "think about such things" and put them "into practice" in their lives (Phil 4:8-9). When they do this, "the God of peace" will be with them.

This is God's calling to each Christian. Lack of purity and holiness in the life of a believer impedes his or her usefulness in God's service. If you want God to use you to reach your children, your holiness of life is not optional.

Phil and Violet learned this the hard way. As leaders of one of their church's home groups they appeared to be happy together and heavily committed to the work of God. What no one knew, however, was that in fact their personal relationship was on the verge of disaster. For reasons neither of them could remember, they had not been communicating at any depth for years. Indeed, both held grudges and resentments against the other, and neither was prepared to make the first move to get things sorted out.

The bubble burst one night during a home group meeting in their living room. During the Bible study, something Phil said triggered a strong verbal response from Vi. The others sat shocked and silent until an experienced counselor in the group, Doug, suggested that he talk privately with the couple outside. As Phil and Vi opened up to him, a sad story emerged of two supposedly sincere Christians whose lives were a sham.

As Doug later reflected on this incident, he began to under-stand why neither of their two children, now in their twenties, came near the church, even though they only lived a couple of blocks away. Despite Phil and Vi's telling everyone that they were praying for their children to return to church, their own lives completely hindered God's working in and through them.

Right Priorities

For God to have full access to a person's life, that individual has to make it clear to him that nothing at all is more important than being in and actively doing God's will. God is not amused by people who say all the right things but do not really mean them. Since he does not practice hypocrisy himself, he does not like seeing it in his people. He uses people who are genuine and sincere and who mean it when they say they love him and want to serve him.

Maybe no follower of Jesus has ever made a more clear-cut expression of commitment to his master than Peter. "Even if all fall away, I will not," he declared in response to Jesus' predic-tion that he would desert Jesus along with his colleagues (see Mk 14:29). For Peter, remaining loyal to Jesus was an absolute priority, even though he did not realize at that moment how hard it would be or how vulnerable he was.

When we read of Peter later filled with the Holy Spirit speak-ing out for his Lord on the Day of Pentecost (see Acts 2:14-40), we see how seriously Jesus took Peter's expression of commit-ment. Admittedly, Peter had let Jesus down badly, but Jesus reinstated him at the Sea of Galilee after the Resurrection. Now full of the divine energy only the Holy Spirit can provide, Peter became God's chosen worker to launch Jesus' church on earth.

Not wasting the years. For years, John had been little more than a pew-warmer in his church. He was there most Sundays but for well over a decade did well at dodging virtually all requests to become actively involved in the church's ministry. He found some comfort and encouragement from the Sunday services, but if asked he would have placed God well down his list of priorities. Sports, home improvements, and his family all came first. Next came his job, which he loathed. God and the church came last on John's list.

John experienced a change of heart, though, when his father was diagnosed with cancer. John found himself reflecting on life more deeply than he had done for years. The reality that his dad might die within a few months provoked John to reconsider what life is all about. Though he had distanced himself from the church for years, his mind kept racing back to what he had learned there as a teenager. Now, all of a sudden, he found that God, faith, and Jesus were relevant to him in a way they had not been for a long time.

As John took a good hard look at his life, he realized how seriously he had allowed his faith to become undermined and eroded. Now that he and his family had a serious need, he knew instinctively that the Lord was calling him back into a relationship such as they used to share. With God and obedience to his will firmly at the top of John's list of priorities again, he knew that the Lord would meet both his deepest needs and those of his family.

Looking back, John now says, "I know I wasted many years in which I could have built up my relationship with God, and I regret it." He still feels bad about the wasted years, but he is deeply reassured that there is now a closeness between him and

God. Furthermore, he knows that because he puts God first, God can, does, and will use him in a variety of ways. These ways include showing God's love to his dying father and communicating the gospel of Jesus to his teenage children.

Making a deep commitment. Another Christian who put God first was Origen, a notable Christian scholar who lived from A.D. 184 to 253. Not only was he familiar with the philosophical debates of his era, but he also undertook rigorous study of the Scriptures, much of which he memorized. To those living around him, his commitment to God was clear. He had "a steely determination of the will to renounce not merely all that is evil but also natural goods if they are obstacles to the attainment of higher ends."[1]

Origen's deep commitment to God was undoubtedly influenced by what had happened when he was eighteen. He had been born to Christian parents in Alexandria, but in A.D. 202, during the persecution by Septimius Severus, his father, Leonides, died as a Christian martyr. This convinced Origen that he needed to put God first in his life. When Decius persecuted Christians, Origen himself was imprisoned and tortured for his faith.

Receptivity to the Power of the Holy Spirit
Of all the messages the Bible communicates to the followers of Jesus, maybe one is clearer than any other: God wants his work on earth to grow and us to be involved in it, but there is no way we can do so without him. As we saw in the previous chapter, he is committed to partnership with us, although he not only provides the resources for his contribution but for ours too. In

short, what he requires of his human partners is their availability and their willingness to use all they have and are (including their minds and mouths) for him and others.

The resources of God emanate from the Holy Spirit. Together with the Father and Son, he had a major role to play in the Creation (see Gn 1:2), and he is shown in Ezekiel's prophecy as being the breath who revitalizes and empowers the people of God (see Ez 37:1-14). It was his descent upon Jesus of Nazareth at his baptism that prepared and energized Jesus for his public ministry (see Mk 1:10). Later it was his coming upon Jesus' disciples in Jerusalem at Pentecost that transformed them from a bunch of frightened witnesses into a powerful force that fearlessly lived for and spoke out for Jesus.

None of us can do much of value for God without the Holy Spirit flowing within us. All the time we think or act at a human level only, we exclude God from being able to work through us. This was a lesson Brenda learned over a few years.

A huge challenge. Having grown up in a solidly Christian family, Brenda was determined to marry a Christian man who, like her father, was dedicated to the Lord. It was after she broke off an increasingly unhappy engagement to a Christian in her church that Brenda met a man at work to whom she was immediately attracted. He had never had any serious contact with a Christian before, so when Brenda started going out with him, she saw him as a challenge. She was determined to see him converted to faith in Christ.

Despite the fact that he remained uninterested and noncommittal about her faith, Brenda found herself falling in love with him. Instinctively, as well as from the teaching of the Bible, she knew that both her family and God would be disappointed if she married him while he remained an unbeliever. She found herself growing closer to him, however, and immediately agreed to marry him when he proposed. Afterward she felt torn and confused.

A decade later Tim, Brenda's husband, still had no interest in her faith, which she had maintained despite some difficult and demanding times. She insisted on going to church each week and often tried to talk to Tim when she came home. He shrugged it off and made it perfectly clear that it was not for him. "I honestly did not know what to do next," she said. "I began to think that nothing and no one would ever get through to him."

Receiving the power. Soon afterward her church had a special ministry weekend when the guest preacher spoke about the way the Holy Spirit can energize believers. Brenda went forward and asked for prayer that she could be an effective witness both to her husband and to their two late-teenage children, both of whom only lived at home on weekends.

As the believers present gathered around and laid hands on her, Brenda knew something was happening to her, although she could not describe it. Nor can she identify what changed at home. All she knows is that she stopped trying so hard and concentrated instead on living close to Jesus each day. The following Christmas she casually asked her family to join her at church for a carol service. You could have knocked her over with a feather when, for the first time in seven years, they all agreed to come.

No one other than God knows quite how, when, and where

the Holy Spirit works. As Jesus said in his conversation with Nicodemus, "The wind blows wherever it pleases. You hear its sound, but you cannot tell where it comes from or where it is going. So it is with everyone born of the Spirit" (Jn 3:8). Only when we become agents through whom the Spirit can flow freely will God be able to use us as his instruments to reach our children.

Live God's Way So That Your Life Makes an Impact on Others

As Brenda learned, it is not our sincerity, determination, or hard work that qualifies us to be used by God, however admirable these qualities may be. God, as I'm sure you recognize by now, wants your children to come to know and love him at least as much as you do. Even though you may not see your grown-up children as often as you used to, God can still use the witness of your life to make an impact on them.

While teaching his followers on a mountainside in Galilee, Jesus showed that if they were to make any serious impact on the world for him, they would need to have similarities to two commonplace things from everyday life: salt and light. Each of these makes its unique contribution to human life, which could not go on without them.

Being salt. Salt has always been important to human beings. It is useful in two particular ways. First, it is a preservative. In Jesus' time, long before the advent of home freezers, salt was precious because of its ability to preserve food. Indeed, even as

I grew up in the 1950s in southern England, I remember seeing jars full of beans encased in salt in my grandmother's pantry. Jesus calls on his friends to live for him, seeking to preserve the godly, just, and wholesome elements of their society when these come under attack.

Salt helps to stop the rot. It is the enemy of decay. When fresh food is enveloped in salt, it remains wholesome and usable. Jesus taught his friends that in a corrupt society, where mankind's sinful nature always has a tendency to pull down levels of morality, they need to be present in the thick of it all, opposing corruption and acting, as author Leon Morris puts it, as "a kind of moral antiseptic."[2]

The second significant feature of salt is its ability to add flavor to food. This reflects another role Christians can have in society. Their lives and witness should not be insipid but full of a Christlike flavor that communicates joy, peace, and unselfishness that others cannot help but notice.

Cooling off. Jolene heard a sermon at church one Sunday on Jesus' call to his friends to be like salt. Because of her own family situation, she immediately thought how the preacher's message related to her husband and children at home. Her husband, Will, had been an active and committed Christian when they married but had gradually cooled off in the years that followed. He said he still believed, but he only went to church on very special occasions.

Their three children had been taken to church each week since they were born and later were all regular attenders at Sunday school. That was until, in their mid-teens, one by one they all indicated that church was for kids and they were past that stage in life now. It broke Jolene's heart when it gradually became obvious that before long she would be the only member of the family still attending church. When their youngest son stopped going at age fifteen, Jolene made the journey alone. "I felt like a failure," she said. "Once five of us from our home went to church each Sunday. Now it's only me."

Three years later she heard the sermon about salt that caught her attention. It made her reflect on her own life and witness. At points she stopped listening to the sermon because she was reflecting on how she had changed the ground rules at home when the children exerted pressure over different issues. Sometimes she felt guilty, thinking she may have failed to stand up adequately for Jesus and the firm, godly principles she had been taught as she grew up in a Christian home. At other times, she felt completely confused.

It took some days and the help of a friend to sort it all out. Jolene knew by then that as a parent she had often made too big an issue out of trivialities. This had not helped relationships with her children, who felt she was inconsistent. She also knew that the joy and peace offered freely to believers were not seen in her life as often as they should be. She only found God's rich peace again when she repented before him and asked for his forgiveness.

Making an impact. The extent to which Christian parents and friends can make an impact on others for God almost defies description. Back in 1865, following a specific call from God, Hudson Taylor founded the China Inland Mission.

The needs of that great country had been drawn to his attention when he was a boy. As he grew up he was deeply influenced by his father, a well-known local Methodist preacher in Yorkshire, England. Hudson also "listened to the preachers as they gathered ... in the parlour behind the Taylors' chemist shop in Cheapside, discussing foreign missions and especially the needs of China."[3] As a five-year-old child he announced, "When I am a man I mean to be a missionary and go to China." It was not until after his conversion at seventeen, however, that he heard what he recognized as a command from God: "Then go for me to China."

As we reflect today on Taylor's highly influential ministry, it is worth recognizing not only his own obedience to God but also the important part his father and his father's colleagues played as they talked together in Bradford about God's worldwide work.

Being light. Jesus also described his friends as "the light of the world" (Mt 5:14). He knew it was his own calling to bring light to the world (see Jn 8:12, a fulfillment of Is 49:6). Just as the moon reflects light from the sun, so in the moral darkness on earth, Jesus' friends are to reflect his glory. People living in darkness will be attracted to the light of Jesus shining brightly through his friends.

This is precisely what God intends to happen within a home as children grow up with at least one Christian parent. Just as "a city on a hill cannot be hidden" (Mt 5:14), neither can the spiritual life that throbs in the lives of Jesus' followers. That is the theory at least.

Before every Christian parent whose children do not yet believe becomes consumed with guilt, however, let us remember one very important thing. Jesus was not the only child in his family, but he was the eldest. We might imagine that to live alongside Jesus as he grew up—to see him pass through adolescence, become a working man and then an itinerant preacher—would have been enough to convince anyone that he was the Son of God. Yet, for whatever reason, his family seems to have misunderstood him, something we presume tells us more about them than it does him.

For instance, John 7:5 tells us that his brothers "did not believe in him," and Mark 3:21 shows that they thought he was mad. At this stage it is clear that his family was not among his followers (see Mt 12:46), although after his crucifixion and resurrection his mother and brothers believed in him (see Acts 1:14). Later James, who became a believer after Jesus' resurrection (see 1 Cor 15:7), went on to become the leader of the Jerusalem church.

Being misunderstood. If Jesus' perfect life did not automatically direct those with whom he lived to his Father in heaven, is it any wonder that our families do not always believe? Not only are we too likely to be misunderstood, our witness also tends to be erratic—unlike that of Jesus. Nevertheless, this in itself does not preclude us from being used by God—as the story of Simon Peter shows.

Jesus called his friends simply to shine for him. He wanted their lives to do what his was doing in first-century Palestine: to light up the darkness around them with the love, joy, peace, justice, and glory of God. As they shone like lighthouses, others would be directed away from danger and guided into a personal relationship with Jesus.

It is because such serious consequences are at stake here that Jesus emphasized the need for his friends to let their light shine.

He makes the obvious point that light is wasted if, having lit a lamp, you hide it under an overturned bowl. Even though it is there, it fails to penetrate the darkness outside (see Mt 5:15). Christians can only make an impact on the world as Jesus did if they boldly live for him wherever they are and whatever they are doing. This includes living for him at home.

Living for Jesus. Two Christians from former generations who did this are Susanna Wesley and the father of Richard Baxter. Susanna, wife of the Reverend Samuel Wesley and mother of his nineteen children, "was a woman of great courage and strength, and ruled her family with firmness and love. Every day she set aside time with each of her children for teaching them the Bible and Prayer Book, and for improving their conduct." When her two famous sons, John and Charles, "left for school in London … she kept in touch by letter, as she did when they went up to Oxford. Concerned always for their well-being, she plied them with good advice and warned them about the assaults of the world." The effects of her ministry are plain to see as we recall the history of the Christian church.[4]

Richard Baxter (1615-91) became a leading Puritan writer, although in his early years he lived with a father who was addicted to gambling. His father, however, was converted "by the bare reading of Scripture in private" when Richard was nine. From then on his life changed, and Richard's father began to live "a godly life. It was because of his father that the young Baxter learned to love the Bible and to appreciate the value of other good books."[5]

Living and witnessing for Christ within the family clearly gives God the opportunity to change lives.

A mixed response. Although by no means every child comes to Christ when raised in a Christian environment, Wendy's experience was also a good one as she and her husband brought up their daughter and son. In their mid-twenties now, their children have moved away from their hometown, but both are committed to the Lord and active in local churches in their respective neighborhoods. Wendy expresses thanks to the Lord for this. "From the beginning," she says, "I sensed that God had his hand on their lives, and apart from a few months when our son's commitment to church was erratic, our two kids have always been keen to follow Jesus."

Other Christian parents, however, have found the effort to bring up their children to be Christians very demanding and thus far unproductive. Jane recalls, "When I first married Jim and our son was on the way, we talked about how we would raise him to be a committed disciple of Jesus, and maybe a preacher or evangelist. Even though in many ways I think we gave him a good spiritual grounding, he left church at thirteen, breaking my heart. My life literally fell apart when at eighteen he was imprisoned for drug abuse, and even now that he's out of jail, he's not really interested in anything spiritual—just fast cars and pretty girls (in that order!)."

What we must understand at this point is that God calls us to witness. When we do this, with a combination of sensitivity and boldness, we can pray that the Holy Spirit will take our feeble words and imperfect lives and use them for God's glory. What we cannot control is the response of others. As Paul wrote to the Christians in Corinth, once we have sowed the seed and watered it, it is God who makes it grow (see 1 Cor 3:6). His calling to us is faithfully and continuously to witness for him.

Unless and until we do so, we cannot expect our children to meet Jesus Christ personally.

Give Yourself to Your Family

Sometimes we ignore or at least overlook the most obvious things. This includes the need for us to show our children that we are wholly committed to them and will always do what is best for them, while also seeking to remain faithful to God. When they understand this, they are more likely to respond warmly to us and respect what we stand for. In this section, then, we look at ways in which you can build and maintain a good relationship with your children.

By Devoting Time to Them

Obviously, where your children now live will determine how much time you can give to them. If they are nearby, you may be able to spend time with them and their families regularly. If their homes are farther away, you will have to be content with phone calls, e-mails, and letters as the main means of communication.

What matters is that they see your commitment to making them a priority in your life. Even though they may be far away and therefore well out of sight, you can prove to them that they are rarely out of mind by sharing your life with them. Regardless of how near or close they may be to God, they need to know their mother and father are deeply interested and concerned about their lives and future.

Jodie and her husband moved into a neighborhood already occupied by many other couples with young children. Almost every husband was employed by one of the several computer firms in the area, and most of the families had moved there from completely different parts of the country. While the friendships between the couples were valued and appreciated, many of these young families badly missed their wider families and the support they would have received from them.

Jodie, however, was far more fortunate than many of the others. Her parents, both committed Christians, had somehow found a helpful balance in the relationship with their daughter, son-in-law, and children. "Mum and Dad phone every week, send the occasional e-mail telling us more detailed news, never miss our birthdays and other anniversaries, and both visit us once or twice a year and invite us all to visit them whenever we want to as well. The clear-cut message we get is that they love us, care about us, but never intrude or push too far. We value that so much," says Jodie. Very often, it is the practical demonstration of Christian love that will make the biggest impact.

By Sharing Their Interests

There are many ways in which we can show we are interested in others. For a parent keen to communicate love and care to their grown-up offspring, one way is to develop an interest in the things they enjoy. Whether it is a sport, a hobby, or a field of study or research, your children will almost certainly value any attempt you make to understand more about their lives and interests.

Of course, this does not mean that if they are dedicated sailors you have to rush out and buy a yacht for yourself. However, if you were to borrow a book on sailing from the local library and read it, trying to grasp some of the terms with which your son or daughter will be familiar, you will be able to discuss sailing with them as never before. This will speak volumes to your children about the way you feel about them. It may also mean that they will reciprocate with questions about *your* interests—which include your involvement in your church.

Your motive in taking this step must be pure and genuine love. If you study up on boxing, stamp collecting, military aircraft, or whatever else it may be simply so they have to ask you about your church, they will soon see through you. This could damage your witness and make it harder for you ever to be able to witness to them in the future.

Let us consider one more thing. If your children do ask about your church, try to speak positively while remaining honest. Remember that every church, while made up of imperfect human beings, belongs to Jesus. Therefore, if you describe in detail a difficult meeting where people squabbled, or you criticize a decision made by the leaders that seems foolish to you, it may hinder the kind of positive impression your children need. Ask God for discernment when you have the opportunity to speak, and ensure that you do not abuse any opportunity you have to talk about God and his work. Your words may make much more impact if they are short and sweet.

By Telling Them You Love Them and Pray for Them

God is love, so there is nothing in the world that is more powerful than love. Regardless of whether your children need to be won to Christ or not, nothing is likely to bond them to you more than your telling them how much you love them. This does not have to be done in a mushy or heavily emotional way. Each relationship is as different as the people who make it up, and not everyone responds well to an emotional approach. What is most important is simply to tell them of your love and concern.

As part of your witness, therefore, tell your children how you feel about them. Whether relationships have been strained or not, use the father in Jesus' parable of the Prodigal Son as your role model (see Lk 15:11-24). His love, care, and willingness to forgive and rebuild relationships can inspire us at any time.

You can use words and actions together to express yourself, but what matters most is the sincerity of what you say and do. Anything that is not transparently genuine will harm both your relationship and your Christian witness. Furthermore, while praying regularly for your children, you can tell them occasionally that this is what you do—not to force a point but simply to let them know that you love them and commend them to your heavenly Father.

As a means of witnessing, Christian greeting cards can be useful also. Some cards with spiritual words and Bible texts are primarily intended for believers to give to one another. But used with discretion, they can be a helpful way of communicating a gentle Christian message to a member of your family who is not yet committed to Jesus Christ.

You Are Not Alone

If one or more of your children are not yet Christians, God wants his love to reach out to them to draw them to himself. As we have seen, he wants to use you to reveal to them the richness of his love and care, but you need to be aware that you may not be the only instrument God will use to reach them.

The Lord has his children located all over the planet. Therefore, while he may have some part for you to play in reaching out to them, he may use others more—especially if you and your children do not live near each other. What matters is that you are as available and accessible as he wants and needs you to be. It is up to him to draw in others according to the plan he perceives will be the most productive.

Meanwhile, as we move on to focus on how God can use you to reach your grandchildren, never give up praying for your children. Your prayers linked to God's power will make a difference.

Six

God Will Help You to Invest Spiritually in Your Grandchildren

As we have seen already, Christian parents often feel frustrated and sad because one or more of their children have not yet responded to the love of God shown in Jesus Christ. Because their own faith means so much to them, these parents want to see their grown-up children turn to Jesus and live each day with a solid, relevant, and meaningful faith. It is hugely disappointing to them that this has not happened yet.

In many cases, though, their children are now married and have offspring of their own, and while their parents may not be Christians, these children are growing up with at least one Christian grandparent. What is more, this grandparent wants to see the whole family turn to God, so the arrival of these children provides a wonderful opportunity for Christian ministry to a new generation.

When Paul wrote to Timothy for the second time, in around A.D. 66-67 from Rome, he encouraged Timothy by referring to the "sincere faith, which first lived in your grandmother Lois and in your mother Eunice and, I am persuaded, now lives in you also" (2 Tm 1:5). According to Acts 16:1, Timothy's mother was a Jewish Christian, although his father was Greek and probably an unbeliever.

What is significant here is that Timothy had a spiritually strong upbringing (see 2 Tm 3:15) and would from a young age have been encouraged to trust in Jesus for himself. That is not to say he was pressured into becoming a Christian, for clearly Paul detects in Timothy a personal and genuine faith. Of his own free will, and probably during Paul's first missionary journey (which is why Paul calls him "my son" in 1 Corinthians 4:17), Timothy had latched on to the fine spiritual heritage that already belonged to his family.

It was never God's plan that what happened in Timothy's life should be a one-time occurrence. Throughout history God has wanted children to be converted to faith in Jesus Christ at least partly through the Christian influence of their families. Clearly, when a child's parents are not Christian themselves, but the grandparents are, this provides an opportunity for the grandparents to let God work through them to reach the newest generation.

If you are a Christian grandparent, you may be asking what you can do in a situation where you have only limited freedom. How can you, like Lois, have the joy of seeing your grandchild come to Christ, even if the child's parents have not yet become Christians themselves? Let us examine five ways in which you can work with God to help this to happen.

By Praying for Your Grandchildren

We have already seen how much difference it makes to pray. Prayer is the means God has given believers to communicate with him. It is the spiritual equivalent of people using the phone to speak to one another. This means that when prayer is real and sincere and the person praying is genuinely trusting in God, the power and resources of almighty God can be released into situations on earth.

If we felt we needed God's help when considering how to reach our grown-up children for Jesus, how much more do we need it when it comes to helping bring our grandchildren to him? We need to remember, though, that without God's active involvement, nothing can or will be accomplished. Part of the problem is that the hands of many grandparents are tied quite tightly as they seek to reach their grandchildren for Christ.

The reason for this may be obvious, but it needs stating all the same. In some cultures today, as in biblical times, family units comprising a number of generations all live together. Consequently, grandparents—and maybe aunts and uncles too—take an active role in bringing up their grandchildren.

In many parts of the world, this is not the pattern at all, however. Because of the fluidity of today's job market, a household comprising two parents and their dependent children often lives far away from the rest of their family.

The effect of this is twofold. First, grandparents are often denied regular access to their grandchildren by the physical distance that separates them. Second, even when parents and children live near the grandparents, the latter frequently only have limited opportunities to see and influence their grandchildren.

Responsibility for the children's upbringing rests firmly with their parents, and any outside interference is often unwelcome.

Prayer Penetrates

This is why prayer is so important. God's power can reach where we cannot. When Peter was in jail awaiting trial and probable execution, the church could get nowhere near him. All they could do was plead with their heavenly Father for his life and future ministry. God heard them and sent his angel to free Peter from the clutches of King Herod (see Acts 12:1-17).

Sherry and Tom have realized the need to pray persistently for their grandchildren. They brought up their own three youngsters over two decades ago, virtually taking it for granted that all of them would become believers because they were raised in a Christian home. With some sadness and regret, they now admit they saw their church as having the prime responsibility for teaching their children Christian truth. "We adopted a kind of laid-back attitude," they say, "but found that one by one our kids left God and the church right out of their lives."

This hit Sherry and Tom hard. When their last child, a daughter, gave up on church, they felt like awful failures, and their own faith went through a time of severe testing. Gradually, however, they came to see that they had failed to take the responsibility for their children's spiritual development and growth as seriously as they should have. One day in their pastor's office, they repented before God and promised they would work in partnership with God to help their grandchildren discover his love.

Now they pray regularly that the Lord will reveal himself to their grandchildren, some of whom live in their own town, while others live a couple hundred miles away. They know distance is not a problem for God and therefore keep asking him to send his Holy Spirit to work actively in that household to bring both the youngsters and their parents to himself. They believe he will, in spite of the fact that it has not yet happened.

By Devoting Yourself to Building Relationships With Your Grandchildren

It is an interesting phenomenon that while relationships between children and their parents can sometimes become strained, those between children and their grandparents are often noted for their freshness, vitality, and depth. Maybe this is a consequence of the grandparents being close family and yet not having any specific responsibility for rearing the children. The result is that both grandparents and grandchildren can relax together and enjoy each other's company without feeling they have to perform.

This was certainly Betty's experience. "I found it liberating to become a grandma and be able to play with the kids without feeling that I needed to police everything they did. Naturally, I kept a careful eye on them, but I certainly didn't hound them like I did my own kids, whom I expected to obey everything I said. The result is that my grandchildren and I have a great relationship and sometimes go out together on days when they're free of studying and work. Being close to them as they have grown up has been one of the most enriching experiences of my life."

This focus on building good relationships between grandparents and grandchildren can be very significant when it comes to reaching out to them with the love of Jesus. Increasingly, evangelists and church leaders today are arguing from experience the truth that Andrew identified centuries ago. When Andrew first met and became enthralled by Jesus, the first person he introduced to him was a member of his family, his brother Simon (see Jn 1:40-42).

Using the Opportunity

Close family relationships are an ideal base from which to share our love for Jesus simply, openly, and honestly. No one denies that crusade evangelism, door-to-door outreach, and open-air preaching are all used by God to draw people to himself. For effectiveness, however, and despite the inevitable disagreements and hiccups that sometimes occur between human beings, surely nothing can beat an ongoing atmosphere of love, care, and trust like that in a close family relationship. This is an ideal environment for sharing God's love, not least because it is felt and sensed in a way that can be very powerful.

Charles Haddon Spurgeon (1834-92), who founded the Baptist college in London where I was privileged to study theology, was brought up by godly parents and grandparents. His grandfather and father were both ministers, and from the time Spurgeon was seven, "his mother lovingly taught her children the Scriptures and prayed for them individually. For Charles she prayed, 'O that my son might live for thee.'"[1]

Charles was fifteen when, in the Primitive Methodist Chapel in Colchester, he responded by faith to the local preacher's message on the text "Look unto me and be ye saved." In one sense, of course, this was the end of a process rather than a snap decision. He had already seen God's love in action through his mother and other members of his family, and spiritually he was like a ripe fruit waiting to be picked.

Making a Sound Investment

This leads us to conclude that there are two very good reasons to invest all you can in your relationships with your grandchildren. First, you love them because they are your children's children and integral members of your family. Second, their parents are not Christians, so you want to build a deeply bonded relationship with them through which you can gently share God's love as they grow up.

This is not to suggest that your relationship with your grandchildren should be heavy and intense. On the contrary, the more relaxed, informal, and full of fun it is, the more likely you are to build a relationship through which God can work. The more your grandchildren are able to see both God's love in you and the real you, the more they are likely to be open to respond when they hear about God's love from you.

Jerry, who lost his wife when he was in his forties, was thrilled when his eldest daughter's first child was born. Although he lived two hours away, he made sure that he visited at least once a month. He got along so well with his daughter and son-in-law that they often invited him to share family vacations and, as a consequence, he got to know his grandson, Martin, extremely well as he was growing up.

"Now I often get to take Martin out to football matches, car racing, or to the seaside," Jerry says. "He and I get on so well, and with him approaching his teenage years, we've found that we share many interests. I certainly don't ram God, Jesus, or the

Bible down his throat, but I try to be natural about my faith, and quite often he raises the subject by asking me some pretty probing questions that I think he stores up until we get to spend some time together."

By Taking Your Grandchildren to Church

For some Christian grandparents, taking their grandchildren to church with them may be a possibility, although it will depend partly on how near they live. In Jerry's case it is not possible on a regular basis, although when Martin comes to stay with him once or twice a year, Jerry takes him along each Sunday.

Martin was eight when he went to church for the first time, and Jerry was a bit apprehensive. "As my daughter and her husband never go near a church, I wasn't sure how Martin would react when he joined me in my regular pew on the first occasion," Jerry reports. "However, he took it all in his stride and loved the kids' part of the service.

"On his third visit he even went to the Sunday school class for his age group without me. He went home full of it, and I got his mum on the phone complaining in a jokey kind of way that I was trying to make her son religious! Not wanting to miss an opportunity, I made some crack about her getting excited about Jesus too, but she didn't reply. The good thing is that I don't think she's anti-Christianity and church anymore—and she used to be!"

Gaining Consent

If your family lives in the same town or area as you do, you may be able to arrange for your grandchildren to accompany you to church. Clearly, this can only happen with their parents' consent, whatever the view of your grandchildren. In fact, it is probably unwise even to broach the possibility of this with your grandchildren until their parents have given the go-ahead.

Martha and Brian brought up their three children in a solidly Christian home and active church. They found it very upsetting when one by one their children rejected church, preferring to live their lives without reference to God. However, they gained their son's approval to start taking his daughter, Jasmine, to church with them most Sundays.

What happened in a crowded pub a couple of months later amused even their son, although he now admits to being embarrassed at the time. "The pub was full, and our son had gone in to have a drink, taking Jasmine with him," Martha reports. "He did not know that having been sitting quietly humming to herself awhile, Jasmine would suddenly start singing, 'Yes, Jesus loves me' at the top of her voice! She had been taught it in Sunday school the previous weekend, and it kept going through her mind!"

Finding Other Ways

In many cases, grandparents will not be able to do the same as Martha and Brian did because their children and their families live too far away. If you are in this situation, does this mean that there is nothing you can do to help your grandchildren learn about Jesus as they grow up? At moments like this, I remember that my mother became a Christian after having been sent as a child to Sunday school at a nearby church by her unbelieving parents. God can still use today what worked then.

Remember, though, that grandparents should almost certainly not take the initiative with this. While you may be sorely tempted to track down an active local church and phone the pastor, asking him to visit your family and to try to recruit your grandchildren for Sunday school, your grown children may well resent this. I am not sure that I would blame them!

There is nothing to stop you, however, from gently suggesting that *they* send the children to a local church one Sunday or, better still, take them along. If they seem unenthused, drop the issue immediately. The alternative would be to ask if they might be interested in developing a connection with a nearby church. If so, you could offer to find out who the pastor is and make the initial contact yourself. What matters is that your children give express approval before you take any action.

By Teaching Your Grandchildren Bible Stories

While the world is full of amazing stories, not only in print but in movies too, there are none more dramatic and captivating than those contained in the Bible. They range in style from gripping, action-packed dramas to tear-jerking romances and everything in between. Furthermore, they are almost certainly bound to capture the attention of your grandchildren.

If your grandchildren's parents are not Christians, however, the chances are that the youngsters will probably not get to hear the stories of the Bible. This is such a shame because the Bible includes rich truth about God that can make a vital impression upon young minds. The more children glean about God in their childhood, the more likely those lessons will remain with them for life.

God has always known this to be true. This is why Moses taught the Israelites:

Love the Lord your God with all your heart and with all your soul and with all your strength. These commandments that I give you today are to be upon your hearts. Impress them on your children. Talk about them when you sit at home and when you walk along the road, when you lie down and when you get up. Tie them as symbols on your hands and bind them on your foreheads. Write them on the doorframes of your houses and on your gates.

DEUTERONOMY 6:5-9

Getting Through to the Children

The question remains: if your grandchildren's parents are not believers, how are the children going to hear God's Word at home? This could happen in one of two ways. First, you read them Bible stories when you see them, or second, you send them books of Bible stories with the hope their parents will read the stories to them or, if not, the children themselves will read them when they are able to do so.

Thankfully, there is a huge selection of children's Bible story-books available around the world today. They are attractively illustrated by gifted artists, and the stories themselves have been rewritten to keep them simple and easy to understand. If your grandchildren have access to books like these, it could help develop in them a love for God and the Scriptures while they are still young.

In addition to the Bible itself, there are numerous children's

Christian songs around, many of which have been recorded on tape or CD. These take biblical truth and express it simply, often in a fun way, sometimes with actions. Next time you are asked to sing such a song in church, try to remember it (or at least its source) so you can teach it to your grandchildren the next time you see them.

Additionally, we need to remember the growing number of Christian videos, DVDs, and CD-ROMs that contain biblical material, some of it for children. You may know whether your family has the equipment to play these often creative and captivating resources. If they have, find out if your grandchildren would be free to use them if you sent the materials to them. At times like this, we should adopt the philosophy of the apostle Paul, whose desire was to work closely with God "so that by all possible means I might save some" (1 Cor 9:22).

Receiving God's Strength

At the end of the day, though, we need to recognize how humanly weak and ill resourced we are when it comes to helping our grandchildren meet Jesus Christ. Writing to the Christians in Corinth, Paul shared the powerful lesson that God had taught him, that there is a limit as to how far you can push and what you can do. That in itself is not a problem, however, for Paul discovered that our weakness provides an opportunity for God to work in a way he cannot if we think we have everything under our control (see 2 Cor 12:7-10).

Dorothy went into her church's women's group with a big smile on her face one day. An hour earlier she had had a phone call from her seven-year-old grandson, Paul, who lives on the other side of the country. The previous week had been

Dorothy's son's birthday, and as he works in a government tax office, she had sent him a birthday card with a humorous cartoon on the front depicting Zacchaeus talking with Jesus.

Paul had not understood the humor in his father's card because he had never heard of Zacchaeus, so he went to school and, with his teacher's help, looked up the account in Luke's Gospel. He wrote about Zacchaeus for a school project he had to complete and then phoned his grandma, Dorothy, to make sure she was familiar with the story too! Dorothy was amazed that so much seemed to have come from so little, but with gratitude to God in her heart, she thanked him for the surprising way his Holy Spirit had been at work.

By Acting With Sensitivity and Gentleness

For Dorothy it all worked out well, but sometimes it does not happen that way. Dorothy felt she knew both her son's sense of humor and his attitude to the Bible well enough to be able to send him a somewhat religious birthday card without it giving offense. Unfortunately, people do sometimes get offended if Christians push too hard or in what is for them the wrong kind of way. This is why sensitivity and gentleness are not optional. Just as soldiers making their way through a minefield have to be extremely careful where they step, so do grandparents who love God and want their grandchildren to love him, too. A lot is at stake.

As a grandparent you have to act sensitively in two respects.

Toward your own children. If the people seeking to influence children are not those who are directly responsible for them, the situation may be perilous. Where those trying to do this are grandparents and the type of influence is religious, the danger levels rise substantially. This is especially true when at least one of the children's parents has rejected Christianity.

The last thing the parents may want is an interfering grandparent on the one hand and a child who recites Bible stories and sings Christian songs all day long on the other. Many parents think the domestic tensions about faith were left behind them when they gave up on church and God as teenagers. Now (if you will forgive the analogy) they can feel as if the same issue has come back again to haunt them.

The fact is this: if you want to be able to show and share the love of Jesus Christ to and with your grandchildren, you will in most cases need their parents' understanding before you can do so. If you discuss it with the parents, they may well demand that you not attempt to pressure the children or edge them into a corner. You will need to agree to these demands, recognizing that this is not the way for Christians to gain new converts anyway. New birth comes from God alone, and our job is to sow seed and water it (see 1 Cor 3:6-7), not try to force growth.

Toward your grandchildren. Even if your grandchildren's parents offer no resistance to your witnessing to their youngsters about your faith, when you do get the opportunity to share with them, you will need to act with sensitivity. A bull-in-a-china-shop approach may well make it harder for the children ultimately to come to faith in Jesus Christ. Put bluntly, few children like being preached at.

To handle this kind of situation you may need plenty of God-given self-control, or else your natural enthusiasm for the Lord could prompt you to push the children too hard. Especially if they are growing up in a home where Jesus is not honored, your grandchildren may find it too much to be lectured on how wonderful it is to experience Jesus' love and how God will meet all their needs if they put their trust in him. If you add in a strong encouragement to go to church each week, that may be the straw that breaks the camel's back. They may reject Christianity forever.

The Drip-Drip Approach

The issue here is not what is and is not true. You can say all the right things and spell out numerous doctrines that you draw directly from the Bible. It is more a question of how to communicate God's truth in a way that twenty-first-century youngsters can accept and digest. Often they need a "drip-drip" approach rather than a deluge.

Randolph only sees his grandmother once or twice a year because she now lives a three-hour flight away. As far back as he can remember, she has been deeply devoted to Jesus, and she has always encouraged him and his brothers and sister to follow Jesus too. Now twenty-one, Randolph dreads going to see her because he knows what she will say to him.

With his vacation looming, Randolph tries to prepare himself for what will happen when Grandma gets him on his own. She will ask him if he has returned to church yet, reprimand him for leaving at fifteen, and then tell him his life will not get anywhere until he hands it over to Jesus Christ. She will follow this up with a reminder that many things young people get into today are sinful in God's eyes, and then encourage him strongly to come to church with her while he is on vacation.

Randolph knows his grandma means well, and deep down he loves her dearly, but he finds her attitude very difficult to handle. Because he is determined to be his own person, he will not let her or anyone else tell him what to believe. Actually, if the truth were known, he does believe in Jesus and once made a commitment to him, although he found church much too boring to continue attending. He would never admit his faith to his grandma, however, and when cornered by her, he opts to remain silent and nod in what he hopes are all the right places.

The method adopted by Randolph's grandmother reminds us how important it is to ensure that we are really communicating with those to whom we speak. It is not enough to be on fire for the Lord and speaking with sincerity. On a one-to-one level, true conversation works much better than lecturing and preaching. Our grandchildren are far more likely to take seriously what we say when we treat them sensitively and with respect and when we think carefully before we speak.

God's Wisdom

What a good thing it is that among the gifts God gives to his church is wisdom (see 1 Cor 12:8). This is exactly what you need as a Christian grandparent when you try to negotiate a tightrope with a danger on either side—the one of being insipid and much too cautious and the other of being too eager and therefore insensitive. There is no room here for a blunt approach that causes offense or for the timidity that makes no impression at all.

Somewhere in the middle is a plan that may allow you the privilege of special opportunities to tell your grandchildren about Jesus without causing a rift in the family. How do we define that middle line? We do so with difficulty, recognizing that what is fine in one situation will cause sparks to fly in another. You can only decide how to proceed after reflecting prayerfully on your family and their background and attitudes. Let God, who gives wisdom to those who lack it (see Jas 1:5), show you what to do.

Your Spiritual Heritage

As we have already seen, God empathizes with your pain, helps you to understand his plans, forgives and heals your past problems, and shines through your witness to your children. The clear message of this chapter is that not only will he do all of these things, but he will also help you to reach your grandchildren with his love.

In chapter 2, we saw that he wants your faith in him to be replicated in your children, their children, and their children's children in years to come. If, therefore, your children—for whatever reason—have so far not responded to God, this is no reason to abandon their children to a Christ-less future.

Psalm 78 argues the importance of families passing on God's truth from one generation to the next.

Listen to this Law, my people, pay attention to what I say; I am going to speak to you in parable and expound the mysteries of our past. What we have heard and known for ourselves, and what our ancestors have told us, must not be withheld from their descendants, but be handed on by us to the next generation; that is: the titles of Yahweh, his power and the miracles he has done. When he issued the decrees for Jacob and instituted a Law in Israel, he gave our ancestors strict orders to teach it to their children; the next generation was to learn it, the children still to be born, and these in their turn were to tell their own children so that they too would put their confidence in God, never forgetting God's achievements, and always keeping his commandments, and not becoming, like their ancestors, a stubborn and unruly generation, a generation with no sincerity of heart, in spirit unfaithful to God.

PSALM 78:1-8, JB

You do not know all the future generations that will be born into your family, many of them after you have gone to heaven. Should Jesus not return for a while, however, God wants your spiritual heritage to live on in the lives of these people at present completely unknown to you. You will, though, meet those who become believers, in many cases for the first time, when you are all united in heaven. What an incentive to invest spiritually in your grandchildren today!

Seven

God Will Use You in Your Church

John and Carol were having a hard time. Following a religious education lesson at school, their youngest child, fifteen-year-old Danny, had announced that he doubted whether Jesus Christ had risen from the dead. In his second serious comment of the week, Danny was now saying that he found church boring and did not intend to go anymore. As Christian parents who had tried with God's help to bring up Danny to believe and trust in Jesus, John and Carol felt sad and under very great pressure.

Simply by exchanging a look, they agreed as Danny was talking that they would not respond immediately. Afterward they debated privately what to do and say, hoping the delay would save them from overreacting and being unnecessarily emotional.

They chose their time to respond very carefully. Danny had just come in from a football game that his team had won. John and Carol asked him to join them and then explained their uneasiness over the things he had said. John spoke calmly and clearly as he told Danny that he and Carol would have much preferred that he sit down and talk through these issues with them. After all, they had always made a practice of discussing important matters openly in their family.

What happened in this household raises some very important issues. Why do so many young people with Christian roots seemingly abandon their faith during their teens? Why do youngsters find church so hard to cope with, and what can frustrated parents do when they find their children rejecting the faith that the parents hold so dear?

God's Way

We have already looked at some of these matters, but the crucial issue of the relationship between today's young people and the Christian church still awaits us. The principle we identified in chapter 2 is relevant here. There we saw that God wants the Christian faith to remain alive within families and to be communicated from one generation to the next.

It is the families in a community that create society as we know it, and the Christian families within it can make a significant impact on the whole. It is God's plan that they should. But God's chief agency for making an impact on the general population is the church of Jesus Christ.

This is made up of representatives of many Christian families cooperating and collaborating together. The church on earth is a huge family unit, comprising people of all ages, races, backgrounds, cultures, and spiritual gifts. The wonder of it, as the apostle Paul observed in his letter to the Christians in Corinth, is that despite its huge diversity, it is essentially one unit (see 1 Cor 12:12).

This is one of the observations John made to his son as they talked. He pointed out to Danny that to be a believer in Jesus (as he had been before) is to be part of a gigantic community of faith that spreads across the world and encompasses millions of people. He said that what binds all these people together is their living relationship with Jesus, and that it is not a trivial matter to withdraw from something like that.

Identifying the Leaks

The fact is, though, that each year hundreds of thousands of young people throughout the world, brought up within Christian families and the Christian church, do precisely what Danny intends to do. The consequence is that the Christian church is deprived of their participation and vibrant input. It can ill afford this leakage.

In this chapter we are concerning ourselves with not only how you can help your adult offspring come to Christ but also how you can work in partnership with God more widely in the church. You may be able to fill a role in your local church that few others could because of your unique circumstances, insight, and concern.

We will focus on three key functions that could be part of your wider service for God. Of course, your main concern is your own family, but regardless of whether or not you find yourself making any headway at present, God can still use you within his church. After all, not all Christians share your spiritual concern for those younger than yourself, and it may be, iron-ically, that God will use you to help others, even though your own family has still not responded to the claims of Christ.

What then can you do to serve God and others within your church?

Try to Understand the Problems
Youngsters Have With Churches

If you have been a Christian for many years, you will have grown used to the ways in which your church works, the style of its worship, and the range of activities that make up its life. The ethos and feel of your church may not have changed much as the decades have passed, although some of the activities will have altered. Furthermore, you feel relatively comfortable with-in your church—which is why you are still there.

If you became a Christian only five years ago, however, it is a fact that even between then and now the *world* has changed substantially. Children growing up today experience a vastly dif-ferent culture and way of life than do those born ten or twenty years ago. There is nothing wrong with this; it is inevitable. Unfortunately, Christians who have been immersed in church life for a long time often fail to recognize this fact.

When the first Christian churches were planted, they were always directly relevant to and in touch with the society in which they were placed. This is clear from the teaching of the apostle Paul, who recognized his own need to keep changing his approach as he roved the known world with the gospel. He needed to present the gospel in one way to win Jews who lived under the law, in another to win those who were not under the law, and yet another to win the weak (see 1 Cor 9:19-23). The churches that emerged as people from these various groups came to believe in Jesus could then be used by God to win others because their style and approach was relevant to them.

Cultural Irrelevance

A great number of churches today seem to live culturally in the past. Their worship style may not have altered radically for as much as a century, even if the style of language has been updated. Most of the music they use comes from the Victorian era, which may suit those accustomed to it; however such music does not attract the unchurched, who are used to contemporary Western culture and music.

Naturally, this includes children and young people brought up by Christian parents and introduced to the Christian faith at a very young age. During their comparatively short lives, these children have spent a lot of time in a variety of environments: at home, often watching a wide range of TV and videos; at school, where their learning has often been creatively inspired; and in leisure pursuits such as sports, music, or other hobbies. Then each Sunday morning they are taken to a church that feels as if they are in a time warp, by parents who want their youngsters to develop a living faith in God in the midst of all the vibrant activity of their busy lives.

When Peter Brierley, Director of *Christian Research*, based in the United Kingdom, analyzed surveys his organization had undertaken, he discovered some worrisome facts. Forty-nine percent of those aged ten to nineteen who attended church in 1979 left over the next ten years. Those who abandoned churchgoing had attended church for nearly four years before giving up. The main reasons they cited for their decision were boring worship services (45 percent), few other young people (36 percent), no activities for young people (24 percent), and old-fashioned services (23 percent).[1]

Unless churches present the unchanging truth about God in a culturally relevant way, youngsters will always have a tendency to view Christianity and church as out-of-date, irrelevant, and boring. You cannot blame them, for it is all they have known. They are not necessarily being intentionally critical, uncaring, or judgmental; it is simply how it seems to them.

Those of us who are older need to understand how different today's world is compared to the one in which we grew up. Youngsters in our postmodern society are taught that religion is a very private matter, has nothing to do with science, and is therefore irrelevant to "real" life, regardless of whether or not your religion seems to meet some personal need of your own. Considering the peer-group pressure over sex and drugs, and the many other things that bombard young people today on all fronts, it is not surprising that many of them struggle to cope with life, which so often appears completely meaningless to them.

The Embarrassment Factor

Rose saw things this way. Her parents had just become Christians when she was born, and they took her to church from her earliest days. She learned the stories of Jesus when her mother read them to her and her teachers in Sunday school taught her. From about the age of ten, however, she began to feel that going to church was not, as she put it, "cool." Some of her school friends laughed at her one Sunday when she was heading there with her dad, and they continued to mock her the next day in front of her classmates.

By the time she was thirteen, she had decided it was OK for her parents to be Christians, but it was not for her. She was into trendy clothes, dancing, and the latest music. In her estimation, Christianity had nothing comparable to offer. Some of the music she heard at church sounded to her as if it had come straight out of Noah's ark!

Rose knew she would have to keep going to church a bit longer to keep her parents happy, but she decided that she would give them no choice once she was fourteen. It was not God but the church she was rejecting when she told her parents the bad news a couple of months after her fourteenth birthday. She explained that it was not only the church in which she had been brought up, it was all churches. After many discussions with her friends, who went to a variety of equally boring churches, Rose had decided they were all as bad as each other.

This is precisely what older Christians have to hear, absorb, and recognize as a valid viewpoint. The message is not directed personally at anyone, and the youngsters do not necessarily intend to cause pain, hurt, or offense to parents or church leaders. It is merely an expression of what many of them feel about church.

Baby Boomers
The Reverend Arnell Arn, a director in the American Baptist Church, has studied the churchgoing tendencies of the 76 million Americans born between 1946 and 1964, commonly referred to as "baby boomers." While many of these people are

today's parents and grandparents, some of Arnell Arn's observations about them apply equally to youngsters growing up today.

> Don't be deceived; baby boomers are a profoundly spiritual generation. Perhaps more than any other group of people, baby boomers are aware that a spiritual world exists.... Their lack of interest in most churches has nothing to do with a lack of interest in God. They like the contents of the Gospel. They just don't like the container—the cultural clothing—they find it wrapped in.[2]

There are many ways in which this can be substantiated. For example, in 1999 a group of eight Baptist churches in western England agreed to contribute to a survey, and one thousand questionnaires were distributed among the congregations. When the contents were analyzed, it was discovered that of the 570 papers returned, 29 percent were from respondents aged sixty-five and above, 40 percent were between the ages of forty and sixty-four, 21 percent were between thirty and forty-four, while a mere 10 percent were under thirty. This provoked an editorial in the British *Baptist Times* entitled, "The Church is now a Senior Citizen—Official," which included the comment:

> Unless in the next couple of decades the churches find some new way of getting the message across convincingly to those in their twenties and thirties, there are going to be even more empty pews (or, these days, chairs) by the time of the 2020s.[3]

Taking a Look Around

No one imagines—least of all me—that the average reader of this book can change the church overnight so that it suddenly becomes attractive, appealing, and "cool" for contemporary young people. What we surely cannot do, however, is sit back and watch as continuing generations of youngsters desert churches around the world. Maybe there is something special that God is calling you to do.

Let us presume that you are a Christian parent whose own child or children have not yet come to faith. Naturally, you are concerned about their long-term spiritual welfare, which is why you are reading this book. My suggestion is, look around your church the first time you can and see how many youngsters currently attend. Then find out how many of them have Christian parents who genuinely care about their becoming part of God's family and kingdom. There may be very few.

The next question you should ask concerns the children and young people who were attending your church, say, five or even ten years ago. How many of them are part of the Christian church (though not necessarily your own) today? My suspicion is that your church, like most others, has been losing young people at a worrisome rate. All too easily we just accept that this is what has always happened and always will. Recognizing that even Jesus lost some followers (see Jn 6:66), this is probably correct. But that does not give us the liberty to pretend it does not matter.

If we accept that God loves every human being and wants everyone "to be saved and to come to a knowledge of the truth" (1 Tim 2:4), then those of us who are aware of what is happening must surely be willing to act to help stop the flow of young people leaving our churches. To be oblivious to it and thus take no action is one thing, but to be aware and then ignore it is surely reprehensible in God's sight. Maybe this is the point at which we need to ask how serious the problem is.

While things may be different where you live, the situation in England where I live is very serious. When the results of the 1998 English Church Attendance Survey were released, Christian statistician Peter Brierley reported that the number of young people up to nineteen attending church in England between 1979 and 1998 had halved.[4] He explains that "half of the overall loss in the 1990s was amongst children under the age of 15 ... while the greatest percentage loss was amongst teenagers, 10 to 19."[5] It is bad enough that on average 2,200 people each week stop attending church in England; it is far worse when you realize that it is the youngsters whom we want so much to see as part of Christ's church in the coming decades who are now deserting it in droves.

Recognizing, then, the extent of the annual loss, how can you or I do anything that will make any difference? Let us look at it like this: if an increasing number of middle-aged and older people in our churches were to begin to understand youngsters better and could see why they find church so hard to cope with, it would be a positive step in the right direction. To do this demands a willingness to try to look at life from a youngster's viewpoint, not just from our own.

Building Bridges

If older Christians would talk with and listen to young people, we would start making some serious headway, especially if they discussed big issues together. As it is, one suspects that all too often adult Christians share fellowship between themselves and—quite unintentionally—ignore children and young people, who then feel ostracized and even unwelcome at church.

None of this is enough in itself, of course, but it would be a start. Tony now admits that he was only in his late twenties when he began to feel uneasy with teenagers. He felt he did not have a clue anymore as to what made them tick, so he gave up leading the youth group in his church. After that he really had no meaningful contact with youngsters for over two decades.

One year his church's home group started to be invaded by young people during the summer, so Tony tried talking with some of them during the refreshments. He was edgy at first, but as time went by he found himself enjoying the stimulating conversations. To broaden his understanding of where these young people were coming from, he began in advance to think about some deeper questions he wanted to ask them.

Within twelve months, Tony's church gained from these encounters. Questions about the teenage youth group had been raised at a church meeting, and some members were suggesting shutting it down. Armed with his fresh understanding of youngsters and a growing passion to see them saved, Tony almost single-handedly took on the doubters and led the church to rededicate itself to ministry among teenagers. It is astounding what just one committed and informed visionary Christian can do for God!

Try to Understand the Misunderstandings That Churches Have With Youngsters

This is just one side of the story, but there is another, as Tony's experience shows. Whether we like it or not, Christians in some churches find young people hard to cope with. They feel that today's youngsters do not dress appropriately for church, have a different agenda for the church, and seem to expect everything to happen in a way that suits them. They might also think that the young people cause damage to expensive church buildings and equipment, leave the place in a mess behind them, and appear to have little respect for those older than themselves.

It is all too easy for established Christians to conclude that it is a mercy these youngsters do not have control over the future direction of the church. "What would the church become under their leadership?" they ask. "Thank God that some mature and responsible people are holding the reins while I'm still here!"

For a whole host of reasons, young people are treated with suspicion, patronized, viewed as lacking experience, and considered naive about life and responsibility. It happens all the time— probably all over the world—but is it fair? This is probably not the right question, for as Scripture shows, age in itself is not the primary factor in determining who has a part to play in God's work on earth.

God Uses Anyone

The Lord viewed Jeremiah's claim as invalid when Jeremiah said he was far too young to be a prophet (see Jer 1:6-7). At the other extreme, God did not consider Abram too old at seventy-five to do something great for him (see Gn 12:4). The message of the Bible is that God will use anyone who is open and available to be his servant and mouthpiece.

While the youngsters in your church may not conform as some older Christians think they should, they are nevertheless part of God's family in the same way as anyone who has placed their trust and faith in Jesus Christ. They can, therefore, become the instruments of God and useful in his service in spite of their inevitable inexperience and naiveté. After all, these characteristics are hardly their fault!

Maybe more mature Christians need to recall their own spiritual pilgrimage—especially if they first believed in Jesus during their childhood or teenage years. I recall with deep appreciation the Christian Endeavour group that met weekly in my home church and of which I was a part. Its purpose was to teach and train young people to take an active part in leading God's work in the present and future. We therefore had full permission to make mistakes as we learned!

Different Perspectives
This broadly correlates with Gemma's experience but contrasts with Jason's. At twenty-one, Gemma has just stopped attending her church's youth group and has instead enrolled for training as a children's group leader. "I have had many happy and beneficial years being led by godly people from our church," she says, "and now I want to help others to be able to get to know Jesus." At thirteen Jason says, "Church does not interest me at all anymore, and I stopped going a couple of months ago. I tried to tell my leaders that I was bored, but who listened? No one."

Earlier we established that your church needs some older people to look at it from the point of view of youngsters. Here we need to recognize that those who can look inward at the church to see how it perceives and treats young people are also required. Are your church's children and young people being viewed in an unreasonable way? If the same people study both sides of this dilemma, so much the better.

Keeping Those Within the Church

A truth that seems obvious yet often overlooked is that children and young people are part of both today's church and tomorrow's church. If we lose them today, it is certain that we will have an uphill struggle trying to win them back later. Rick Warren, the pastor of one of America's fastest-growing churches, estimates that it takes "about five times more energy to reactivate a disgruntled or carnal member than it does to win a receptive unbeliever."[6] Clearly, we need to pray and work hard to keep those we already have.

We will do this more successfully when we recognize humbly and sincerely that those of us who are older have not necessarily got it all right, while the youngsters have got it all wrong. God wants us to see that he has plans for them and needs their vitality, enthusiasm, commitment, energy, strengths (and weaknesses) so he can set to work and make them increasingly more like his Son, Jesus. After all, is he not doing this with us?

Older Christians who have their eyes open to the issues that surround ministry to children and young people in the church will always be of great value in the work of God in their community. So much the better if they also have the ear of their church's leadership or are even a part of it. Churches will only retain the youngsters they have and gain others if they are prepared to face up to contemporary issues and then be prayerful and creative in the way they handle them. Letting young people continue to flood out of our churches is surely not an option.

Understanding Young People

What can churches do? For a start, some Christians at least could try to understand the setting in which youngsters grow up today and how they tend to spend their time:

- One teenager in six smokes, and one in fourteen has tried drugs.
- Crime among teenagers is increasing, especially in males.
- Personal income rises rapidly between fifteen and twenty and is spent on alcohol, clothes, and eating out (in that order).
- Getting a job is a key priority for the average teenager.
- Twelve percent of the 3,900 suicides in England and Wales in 1991 were committed by those aged 15-24.
- Seven percent of women conceive before the age of twenty, and 2.5 percent will have an abortion.
- The main teenage after-school activities are watching television (92 percent), listening to music (86 percent), and doing homework (82 percent).
- Other activities include watching videos (64 percent), hobbies (58 percent), playing sports (57 percent), and computer games (47 percent).
- Favorite places to go for school teenagers are movies (51 percent), discos (36 percent), and games arcades (27 percent); and for church teenagers, church activities (53 percent), movies (46 percent), and youth clubs (44 percent).
- Fourteen percent of churched sixteen-year-olds have lost their virginity, 43 percent by the age of nineteen, whereas 41 percent of unchurched sixteen-year-olds have done likewise.[7]

- In a strong consumer culture, youngsters gather around brand names such as Nike, Apple Macintosh, Nintendo, and Calvin Klein. According to French sociologist Michel Maffelosi, this is how postmodern "tribal groupings cohere on the basis of their own minor values."[8]

Much of this is completely different from the world in which those of us over forty grew up. Culture has changed, whether we like it or not. Indeed, many of the things that fill the time of today's youngsters had not even been invented when some of us were growing up! For this reason, we often do not understand the pressures and tensions of today's teenagers.

Able and Willing to Understand

I do not believe that God is calling forty-, fifty-, sixty-, and seventy-year-old Christians to dress up in the latest trendy clothes and go spend an evening at a local disco in order to get the feel of how today's young people tick. Thankfully, there are other ways. What is important is that in every church there are those who, though distanced from today's young people by their age, are nevertheless able and willing to understand the kind of world in which youngsters live and the pressures they face.

Who these Christians are in each church does not matter. Sometimes they will be the youth leaders, but at other times they may be concerned parents whose own children have not yet come to faith. Whoever they are, they will be concerned that the Christian church does all it possibly can to ensure that those still within its community remain there. Such Christians will probably have hearts burning with a passion to see youngsters brought to Christ—and passion with vision drives people to do extraordinary things in God's service.

Often the role of these people may be to monitor the children's and youth ministry of their church and then do their best to ensure that the youth leaders who serve them are meeting the youngsters' needs. Understanding ...

- how the style of church life tends to alienate young people;
- how some Christians' attitudes to youngsters can prove unhelpful;
- at least some facets of contemporary youth culture;

... will enable these Christians to pray and work hard for each successive generation that becomes part of their church. As God works through them, their commitment can make a huge difference in the impact of the gospel in their community.

Consider Investing in the Youth Ministry of Your Church

Finally, without in any way denigrating what has been said so far, we need to recall the nature of the God we serve. He is a true activist. While there is always a need for accurate observation and careful assessment, throughout history God has been committed to making good things happen.

The collaboration of Father, Son, and Holy Spirit in the work of creation is a case in point, as was God's intervention in the life of Moses so that God could use him as the leader who brought the Israelites out of bondage in Egypt. However, of all the significant events described in the Bible that were important to human history, none surpasses the coming of Jesus of Nazareth. He was God himself in human form, and he came to pay the penalty for the sins of the human race and to overcome evil forever.

God believes in taking the initiative, acting positively and decisively in order to tackle problems head-on. Where he sees a need, he does not sit back and wait for someone else to act. Furthermore, since the emergence of the Christian church on earth, he looks to Christians, his servants, to respond to the guidance provided by the Holy Spirit and to take fresh initiatives on his behalf.

This means that when God sees a situation in our world that causes him concern, he wants to improve it. Where he sees the children of Christian parents not yet in a relationship with him despite their parents' godly influence, the Almighty wants things to change for the better. To ensure that it does, he sends his Holy Spirit to work in various strategic ways.

Prayer and Action

First, as we have seen already, God invites Christian parents to work in partnership with him through prayer and action. Their concern is for their now grown-up children to come to know him. As they pray and take action, and as he leads them by his Holy Spirit, so he works in and through their lives. After all, God wants the children of Christians in his kingdom at least as much as their parents do!

Sharon is relieved at this. Her daughter Tanya, now twenty-three, very nearly became a Christian at seventeen but fell in love and was distracted from her emerging faith in God. Sharon is thankful to God for a great deal, but not many things surpass her gratitude for her growing belief that ultimately Tanya will come to know Jesus personally. Having prayed daily for Tanya for over ten years, Sharon could easily be discouraged. But her conviction is deepening that God is quietly and deliberately at work in her daughter's life.

Second, God lays a burden on the hearts and minds of some believing parents to become involved in helping other youngsters who are now connected with the church. In other words, their own children may have left the church and for the time being are ignoring God's claims on their lives, but there is an opportunity to share God's love with today's teenagers who *are* at church and who are still very much open to being influenced by the gospel.

Using the Opportunities

Of course, different churches work in different ways, and the range of opportunities for service will vary from one to another. In some, the church's leadership will be looking for those who can teach a Sunday school class. In others, they will be keen to find leaders who can work in a more informal club-based environment with the kids, while another church may want sports instructors or specialists in outdoor pursuits. The range of possibilities is limitless. What matters is that each church makes the best use of all the opportunities that exist to introduce children and young people to Jesus.

Maybe God is calling you to serve him in some active way with youngsters at the church you attend while you continue to pray for your own children. Sharon senses that this is the way God is guiding her. In her teens, she was her school's star swimmer, and when she finished competitive swimming, she took a number of courses to learn how to train others. It has been a decade since Sharon was actively involved in swimming training, but now, in her early forties, she has enrolled for some refresher courses so she can offer her services to the youngsters in her church who enjoy water sports and are eager to develop their skills. Sharon sees this as a great way to get alongside teenagers and build a relationship with them that can be a basis for sharing the gospel with them later.

Whatever your gifts, your interests, and your available time, God has a part you can play in helping children or young people in your church. They need Christ whether they know it or not. With prayer, encouragement, and opportunities to both hear the gospel and see it being lived, there is every likelihood that many of them could turn to Jesus and become spiritually vibrant men and women of God in the years ahead. Maybe God wants you to have the privilege of working with some of them and the joy of seeing them turn to him.

Looking Ahead

Many pages back, I began by focusing on the pain you feel because your offspring do not know Jesus yet. I am ending with encouragement for you to trust God to do miracles in the days ahead and to become involved with him to such an extent that he uses you as his partner to bring people to himself. These may be your own youngsters about whom you care deeply, or they may be the children of other parents whom God allows you to get to know and with whom you can share his love.

Finally, let me share a personal word with you. Dr. Larry Crabb tells how as a child he used to have a problem with stuttering. One Sunday morning in a church service, he sensed pressure from the congregation that he should pray out loud during Holy Communion. He was so petrified that he both stuttered and got his theology confused. As he sat down, he dared only look at the floor because of his total embarrassment.

When the service ended, he headed straight for the door, but an older Christian man intercepted him. Larry was sure the man was going to reprimand him, but to his surprise, the man said, "Larry, there's one thing I want you to know. Whatever you do for the Lord, I'm behind you one thousand percent." The man then walked away.[9]

You may make some mistakes too, but I encourage you to offer yourself fully to God and let him use you, even if you do not get it right every time. What is important is that the God who has saved you and brought you into his family can reveal himself and his love through you to others. Who knows how many people may be drawn into his kingdom as God works through you next year, next month, next week, or even today?

Notes

ONE
God Will Empathize With Your Pain

1. Larry Crabb, *Men and Women* (London: Marshall Pickering, 1991), 61.

TWO
God Will Help You to Understand His Plans

1. From *Finding Faith in 1994*, a survey undertaken on behalf of *Churches Together in England* and quoted in *12 Things ... To Wake Up To!* (London: Christian Research Association, 1999), 9.
2. John C. Pollock, *Shaftesbury* (Oxford: Lion, 1990), 20-21.
3. John C. Pollock, "Billy Graham," from *Great Leaders of the Christian Church*, ed. John D. Woodbridge (Chicago: Moody Press, 1988), 368.

THREE
God Will Forgive and Heal Past Problems

1. Sheila Bridge, *The Art of Imperfect Parenting* (London: Hodder and Stoughton, 1995), 7.
2. Geoffrey Hanks, *70 Great Christians* (Fearn, Scotland: Christian Focus, 1998), 50.
3. Metropolitan Anthony of Sourozh, *School of Prayer* (London: Darton, Longman, and Todd, 1999), 33-34.

FOUR
God Will Work Through You As You Persistently Pray

1. *Finding Faith in 1994,* 9.
2. Peter Lord, *When Your Child Wanders From God* (Grand Rapids, Mich.: Spire, 1998), 17-18.
3. Story and quotations taken from *Artist Biography of Richard Jon Smith,* (Bletchley, England: Word Music, 1999).

FIVE
God Will Shine Through Your Witness

1. Henry Chadwick, *The Early Church* (Harmondsworth, England: Penguin, 1967), 100.
2. Leon Morris, *The Gospel According to Matthew* (Grand Rapids, Mich.: InterVarsity, 1992), 104.
3. Hanks, 185.
4. Hanks, 171.
5. Hanks, 143.

SIX
God Will Help You to Invest Spiritually in Your Grandchildren

1. Hanks, 250.

SEVEN
God Will Use You in Your Church

1. Peter Brierley, *Reaching and Keeping Teenagers* (Tunbridge Wells, England: MARC, 1993), 89-125.
2. Arnell P.C. Arn, "Baby Boomers...Can We Reach Them?" *The Good News Link,* 15, No. 2 (Summer 1991).
3. "The Church is Now a Senior Citizen–Official," *Baptist Times* (Didcot, England), October 14, 1999, 1-2; October 21, 1999, 5.
4. Peter Brierley, *The Tide is Running Out* (London, England: Christian Research, 2000), 94.
5. Brierley, 129.

6. Rick Warren, *The Purpose Driven Church* (Grand Rapids, Mich.: Zondervan, 1995), 183.
7. All statistics in this paragraph up to this point from: Brierley, *Reaching and Keeping Teenagers,* 56, 88.
8. Chris Rojek, *Decentring Leisure* (Sage), as quoted by Graham Cray in "Youth Congregations—The Best Biblical Bridge?" *Youthwork* (August 1999), 14.
9. Lawrence J. Crabb and D. Allender, *Encouragement: The Key to Caring* (New Malden, England: Navpress, 1986), 24-25.

Further Reading

The following is a list of titles that cover many of the subjects raised in this book.

Bridge, Donald. *When Christians Doubt.* London: MARC Europe, 1987.

Bridge, Sheila. *The Art of Imperfect Parenting.* London: Hodder and Stoughton, 1995.

Brierley, Peter. *Reaching and Keeping Teenagers.* Tunbridge Wells, England: MARC, 1993.

Christenson, Evelyn. *What Happens When We Pray for Our Families.* Amersham-on-the-Hill: Scripture, 1992.

Coffen, Richard W. *When God's Heart Breaks.* Hagerstown, Penn.: Review and Herald, 1997.

Crabb, Larry. *Men and Women.* London: Marshall Pickering, 1991.

Crabb, Lawrence J. and D. Allender. *Encouragement: The Key to Caring.* New Malden: NavPress, 1986.

Dunn, Ronald. *Don't Just Stand There ... Pray Something!* Amersham-on-the-Hill: Scripture, 1992.

Grant, George. *The Family Under Siege.* Minneapolis: Bethany, 1994.

Kesler, Jay. *Grandparenting: The Agony and the Ecstasy.* London: Hodder and Stoughton, 1994.

Larcombe, Jennifer Rees. *Where Have You Gone, God?* London: Hodder and Stoughton, 1989.

McCallum, Dennis, ed. *The Death of Truth.* Minneapolis: Bethany, 1996.

Lord, Peter. *When Your Child Wanders From God.* Grand Rapids, Mich.: Spire, 1998.

McGrath, Alister. *A Journey Through Suffering.* London: Hodder and Stoughton, 1992.

Mayes, Gary. *How to Trust God When Life Doesn't Make Sense.* Leicester, England: Crossway, 1995. Originally published as *Now What!* Wheaton, Ill.: Crossway.

Metropolitan Anthony of Sourozh. *School of Prayer.* London: Darton, Longman, and Todd, 1999.

Omartian, Stormie. *The Power of a Praying Parent.* Eugene, Ore.: Harvest, 1995.

Pearson, Althea. *Growing Through Loss and Grief.* London: Marshall Pickering, 1994.

Robinson, Martin. *The Faith of the Unbeliever.* Crowborough, England: Monarch, 1994.

Short, Claire. *Parenting Teenagers.* Milton Keynes: Scripture Union, 1996.

Veith, Gene Edward. *Postmodern Times: A Christian Guide to Contemporary Thought and Culture.* Wheaton, Ill.: Crossway, 1994.

Warren, Rick. *The Purpose Driven Church.* Grand Rapids, Mich.: Zondervan, 1995.

Watkins, William D. *The New Absolutes.* Minneapolis: Bethany, 1996.

Woolmer, John. *Thinking Clearly About Prayer.* Crowborough, England: Monarch, 1997.

Scripture Index

Genesis 1:2 94
Genesis 3:16-19 88
Genesis 3:16-23 28
Genesis 3:21 33
Genesis 4:6-7 33
Genesis 5:32 70
Genesis 6:6 28
Genesis 6:6-7 70
Genesis 6:8 70
Genesis 6:9 . . . . 70, 71
Genesis 6:22 71
Genesis 7:1 34
Genesis 9:25-27 71
Genesis 11:8 74
Genesis 11:9 28
Genesis 12:1 74
Genesis 12:1-3 61
Genesis 12:3 85
Genesis 12:4 138
Genesis 15:6 74
Genesis 18:20 28
Genesis 20:1-13 61
Genesis 27:1-29 62
Genesis 28:10-17 62

Exodus 3:11 87
Exdus 4:13 87
Exodus 32:10 28
Exodus 32:35 28
Exodus 34:29 63

Deuteronomy 6:5-9 119

Judges 13:2-25 36

1 Samuel 3:2-10 36

1 Samuel 16:1-13 36

2 Samuel 12:1-10 88

Psalm 24:4 88
Psalm 51 . . . . 36, 58
Psalm 78:1-8 125

Proverbs 22:6 9

Isaiah 49:6 99
Isaiah 56:7 86

Jeremiah 1:1 37
Jeremiah 1:6 87
Jeremiah 1:6-7 138

Ezekiel 37:1-14 94

Hosea 11:1-9 29

Matthew 1:1-17 40
Matthew 5:14 99
Matthew 5:15 101
Matthew 5:21-48 89
Matthew 7:7-8 82
Matthew 12:46 100
Matthew 17:20-21 69
Matthew 19:26 25
Matthew 21:12-13 29
Matthew 27:46 29
Matthew 28:19 86

Mark 1:10 94
Mark 3:21 100
Mark 5:21-43 78

Mark 9:2-29. 78
Mark 14:29 91

Luke 1:13-17. 37
Luke 3:7 37
Luke 4:32 79
Luke 5:16 79
Luke 6:12 79
Luke 9:1-6. 79
Luke 9:18 79
Luke 11:5-8. 82
Luke 15:11-24. 106

John 1:1-4. 29
John 1:40-42. 114
John 3:8 96
John 6:66 135
John 7:5 100
John 8:12 99

Acts 1:4-5 77
Acts 1:8. 86
Acts 1:14. . . . . 77, 100
Acts 2:14-40 91
Acts 3:1. 77
Acts 5:1-11 90
Acts 8:3. 62
Acts 9:1-2 62
Acts 9:3-9 62
Acts 12:1-17 112
Acts 16:1 110

1 Corinthians 3:6. 102
1 Corinthians 3:6-7 122
1 Corinthians 4:17. 110
1 Corinthians 9:19-23 131
1 Corinthians 9:22. 120
1 Corinthians 12:8. 124
1 Corinthians 12:12. 129

1 Corinthians 15:7. 100

2 Corinthians 12:7-10 120

Philippians 4:8-9 90

1 Timothy 1:2 38
1 Timothy 2:4 135

2 Timothy 1:5 . . . . 38, 110
2 Timothy 3:15 110

Hebrews 9:15 58
Hebrews 11:1 76
Hebrews 11:8 74

James 1:5. 125